The Adventures
of an
Alaskan
Game Warden

By Al Huba

Autograph Page

Acknowledgements

I would like to acknowledge the men of the Alaska Department of Fish and Game who served with me and to those who bravely blazed the trail before me. I remain deeply indebted to them.

Al Huba

Table of Contents

Table of Contents

Introduction

Have you ever dreamed of something that you really wanted to do? It may have been something that you just couldn't shake; it seemed to always be with you. You were in love with it and soon it was no longer just a dream; it became a vision and a passion. It is all too easy to lose that passion- stuff gets in the way. Please don't let it; for when you are on death's bed it is a sorrowful thing to hear a raspy voice say, "I wish I would have….." This book may have just been written for you.

As far back as I can remember I always wanted to be a game warden, especially one in Alaska. It is pretty evident where that strong desire came from. I can recall reading dozens of Outdoor Life and Field & Stream magazines that my father had collected over the years. Dad was the consummate outdoorsman –a rugged steelworker wearing a dented metal hat one day and the next donning a floppy, fish- stained canvas fishing hat pierced with a hundred dry flies. Most of my spare time was spent reading stories by Frank Dufresne and Jack O'Connor about hunting and fishing in Alaska.

To be afraid to dream today is perhaps a precursor to being afraid to really live tomorrow. I can remember at 14 dreaming about Alaska, pretending I was driving there. Dad had just purchased a 1941 Buick convertible that was the talk of the neighborhood. Dad left the keys in the car which was not unusual in that day. I had no driving lessons under my belt yet but in my passion to reach Alaska I cautiously turned the key, depressed what I believed was the clutch, dropped it some gear, popped the clutch and lurched forward, jumping and bucking across the yard. Narrowly missing the bird bath and flower garden the Buick and I came to an abrupt stop inches short of hitting my house. Well, it was a start; only 5000 miles and a few yards to reach "The Last Frontier". When I explained it later to Dad he came over and patted me on the shoulder and said something to affect that: "Maybe you should take me along next time."

Over the next 10 years or so I kept my dream alive concerning Alaska, even though after graduating from high school, I departed to college on a path that seemed to deviate from my dream. I could remember being in my junior year in 1963 at Penn State in the engineering program, hating it and thinking about what it would be like to live in Alaska. The year before, a good friend of mine, Ron, and I met in the Army at Fort Knox. He departed for Alaska in '63 and I quit college and went to work for Armco Steel soon after. In 1964 you could earn the unbelievable sum of six dollars an hour working construction in Alaska while the steel mill wage was about two dollars and fifty cents. Many lunch hours were spent speculating on how a generational steel mill bum could somehow break loose from the bonds that held him there. More than doubling ones wage was certainly an incentive, but mine ran much deeper. I was in love with something I had never met. I was totally infatuated with a place. I didn't just want to go there, I had to go there-Alaska!

My friends soon bid me farewell and I and left Butler, Pa. in a 1963 Jeep Wagoneer on March 22, 1966. The journey from Western Pennsylvania to Montana was quite uneventful, but it was certainly not that way after leaving Montana. Soon I embarked on the Alaska Highway, some 1200 miles of gravel road that was built for military purposes in the mid-1940s. It was now a venue for public transportation hosting hundreds of truckers, tourists and fortune hunters like myself. While driving, I was so excited that I could hardly sleep, so I drove almost 24 hours a day, catching a wink or two along the way. The scenery was spectacular and I drank in the sights like a thirsty pioneer. This was surely a taste of Heaven I thought. Little did I know what awaited me just a few miles up the road.

As I was going over the summit of the highest point on the Alaska Highway, a place called Steamboat Mountain, I heard a loud crack from the rear of the Jeep. The left rear part of the axle had broken off causing the wheel assembly to jam itself underneath the carriage of the vehicle. This slowed the speed down to 40 plus miles an hour. That doesn't seem very fast, but when you're going down a steep mountain, with no guard rails and sheer drop of some thousand feet, it becomes verrrry exciting. Somehow I made it down the mountain and was shaking noticeably when a Royal Canadian Mounted Policeman (RCMP) pulled up to my rear. He announced that he had all the broken parts from my vehicle in a box if I wanted them. I said yes, not sure what I was going to do with them. The Mountie courteously suggested that he drive me to the nearest mechanic which luckily was only a couple of miles down the road.

The mechanic was also the owner, with his wife, of the Circle T Restaurant, filing station and garage. While he was repairing the Jeep I worked off my room and board by running errands and delivering small quantities of fuel to their customers. I was thankful to have food and shelter in a land foreign to me. I was also delighted to lie down at night and hear the wolves howl from just across the Toad River- just like it was in *Outdoor Life* and *Field and Stream*.

A few days later the parts for the Jeep arrived by bus from Vancouver, B.C. The mechanic quickly and expertly assembled the parts and I was finally on my way north. I regretted that I had just spent half of my savings on repairs but had no choice in the matter. I later learned that Circle T was quite benevolent to me and could have charged me much more than the 250.00. I now had to make up for lost time as I promised my friends that I would most certainly be in Anchorage before Easter. It was now early Thursday morning and I had 1200 miles to go, much of it gravel.

I purposed in my heart that if I drove without sleeping I could make it to Anchorage by late Saturday. The trip was rather uneventful except for an incident that occurred near the Canadian/ Alaskan border close to the little village of Tok. Rounding a turn I noticed what appeared to be a large cat slowly crossing the road. It turned out to be a very large lynx carrying a beautiful prime winter coat of fur. Being a hunter and trapper, it was difficult not to claim this creature as my first kill in Alaska. I settled rather for a few Kodak special moments.

The weather was cooperative and I found myself on the outskirts of the big city in late morning on Saturday, Easter eve 1966. I had one more point of business to take care of before meeting up with my friends. I hadn't eaten in 24 hours and could eat a porcupine, quills and all. I had heard back home in Pa. that a local couple was managing a diner in Anchorage and if I had a chance I should drop in. The name of the diner was the Lucky Wishbone. After settling in on a stool at the counter I asked for the managers from Pa. but it was their day off.

A slight silver-haired gentleman seated nearby sensed my disappointment, came over and asked if I was new in town. I replied that I was. He politely introduced himself as Bill Egan. Lady Fortune must have been smiling at me for the first person that I met in Alaska turned out to be none other than the governor himself! In some ways, Alaska has always remained small.

Getting a job was my next order of business. Fortunately, I had a degree in electrical technology which made the search easier. I soon found myself working for Honeywell Inc. as a draftsman. The pay was substantial and I soon settled down to a fresh life in the Land of the Midnight Sun. However, life in Anchorage did not somehow measure up to the dreams that I had of Alaska. Sure, I had the weekend fishing sojourns to the Kenai Peninsula and north along the Glenn highway, but there was still something missing. Could it possibly be that I had forgotten about being a game warden?

In 1965, the year before I had left Pa., I had taken a home study course on learning how to be conservation officer. I finished with an excellent grade and was encouraged to send out some letters to possible employers. One letter and resume that I sent was to the Alaska Dept. of Fish and Game. I didn't hear back from them. Providentially, in the fall of 1968 while employed by Honeywell, I received a letter from the ADF& G asking if I was still interested in interviewing for the position of Wildlife Protection Officer. They also apologized for the long delay explaining that my letter of 1965 was inadvertently delivered to a fellow agency, the Federal Fish and Wildlife Service!

Part One

The Rookie Works Close to Home

Chapter One

Little Big Gun

"Al, there's a phone call for you," reported my secretary at Honeywell. It was the Alaska Department of Fish and Game (ADF&G) asking when I could come in for an interview. I was now a draftsman, how do I make the transition to even talking about game warden stuff? I told them that I would come in at their convenience. Are you kidding me? I would have swum the Bering Straits in my Speedos for this chance! The interview, I was informed, would consist solely of an oral exam. It seemed much too easy.

The interview room looked more like an interrogation room. For the next two hours I felt like I was being….. well…. interrogated! It was the moment of truth for me- probing question after probing question. "Will you, if hired, be willing to live in substandard housing?" I immediately answered, "yes!" I answered too quickly I thought, but at this point I would have lied to the Pope. Then came the question that separates the men from the boys: "If you knew your mother had committed a fish and game violation, what would you do"? I couldn't let this one go. Fighting to keep a straight face, I calmly replied, "I would call for a backup." I got the job.

The next few weeks were spent meeting scores of people from the different offices within the Department. These were the folks that I would be working with for the next several years; Sport Fisheries, Commercial Fisheries, Big and Small Game and Waterfowl -biologists and techs of all sorts. As a good warden it was imperative that I develop a strong working relationship with these people- and I did.

I was assigned to a different officer each week to learn the ropes. Some were seasoned officers with decades of experience while others were my senior by only a few months. Being the low guy on the totem pole won me the privilege of picking up the animal road kills. These usually were moose that had encounters with vehicles at night. It was not unusual to get 2 or more per night. It was my duty to locate the moose encounter and to get the animal off the road as soon as possible. The animal was not always dead when I arrived so I then had to dispatch it. My weapon of choice was a 410 gauge Remington shotgun with a rifled slug. If placed properly it did the job. I next had to eviscerate the animal, skin and then quarter it. The process normally took about 2 hours; my first one having taken about twice that long. I had a lot of practice dressing out those white tails back in Pa. But these critters were another story- they were 8 to 10 times as large. After the process was finished I would then call a local men's shelter and they would come and pick it up. They were very thankful, for the average moose would provide them with 500 to 600 lbs. of fresh meat.

One afternoon at approximately 5PM I received a call from the gate at Fort Richardson Army Post that a large cow moose had just been hit by a vehicle. By the time that I arrived, a small crowd had gathered watching the crippled cow moose slowly make its way into the brush. Just before it disappeared I noticed that its left front leg was broken. The moose had to be killed. I placed a slug into the gun and cautiously stepped into the forest. Slowly I crept forward, my heart pounding, recalling that moose kill more people in Alaska than bears do....than **bears** do.... than **bears** do.

Soon there she was about 15 yards in front of me. Her hackles were standing up on her back, a clear signal that I had better not come one step closer. I waited patiently for her to turn her head so I could place the shot precisely behind her ear. That would be a quick and merciful kill. Slowly I raised the gun and waited- there it was, squeeze slowly. Click! What? – a misfire. I quickly reloaded. Click again. I cracked the gun open and discovered a broken firing pin! The gun was now worthless. By now the small crowd had followed me into the forest and was watching my every move. I reached for my backup piece- a 2 ½ inch snub- nosed 38 cal. Colt handgun.

It was my personal weapon, not exactly what you would call a big game gun. The moose was getting very fidgety and I knew that at any second she could charge. Neither I nor the people behind me would have a chance against her lethal hooves. Slowly I once again raised my gun, albeit small, and waited for the head turn. I waited- 10 seconds, 15, 20, an eternity. There! - The opening behind the ear.

Pop! Down she went with a crash. She shook for a few seconds and then all was quiet. Out of the crowd came a lone clap, then another and another –a tribute to one scared warden and one dead moose. As I strode forward to begin the dirty job of dressing out the fallen moose I overheard one of the observers comment: "Yah, that handgun that F&G uses now; it's one of those 44 magnums and I think he has a silencer on it." I didn't offer the truth but hoped that his ignorance would be blissful.

Chapter Two

Moose Versus GI

After a long night on patrol I could have really used some sleep. But when duty beckons the warden must respond. It was a call from the Alaska State Troopers dispatcher informing me that a Trooper needed my help in the Muldoon area of town. I told her that I would be there in 15 minutes. A thick fog had engulfed the Anchorage area during the night which made driving precarious. Arriving later than the anticipated 15 minutes I spotted the familiar flashing red light along the side of the road. The scene was a grisly one. A mid-sized sedan was in the ditch beside the road with its roof peeled back like an open sardine can. The Trooper waved me closer and quickly explained the details.

The driver was a GI from Ft. Richardson Army Base who was living off base. He was returning to work that morning at approximately 6:30 AM when he had an encounter with a large cow moose. Due to the dense fog the driver never saw the moose on the highway and struck it broad side without braking. The vehicle apparently traveled under the body of the moose causing the animal to roll over the roof and peel the roof back with it. Since I didn't see the driver I asked the Trooper where the driver was and he replied, "Do you really want to know?" I replied in the affirmative. He then pointed out to me that the torso of the GI's body was in the front seat and his head was in the rear. I felt a rift in my stomach and decided to tend to my business while the Trooper tended to his. In no way would I have wanted to trade places with him.

The moose was nowhere to be seen. The trooper now would not want to trade places with me. A crippled moose somewhere in a thick fog was not exactly the best way to start a day. I soon found a faint blood trail leading into a thin stand of black spruce. The sun was starting to peak over the Chugach Mountains which would make seeing easier. The cow had not lain down – that was a good sign. She was slowly walking through the woods; I couldn't hear her because of the deep snow but I knew she was close by- the ravens were squawking just ahead of me. Suddenly there she was, 25 yards away. Not seeing me, her ears were pivoting back and forth trying to detect my sound, her keen nose attempting to pick up my scent. I carefully observed the moose for the next half hour and after seeing her start to browse on some birch twigs decided to leave her alone for the time being. Subsequent checks on the injured animal over the next few days revealed her feeding normally and the stools she passed were almost blood free- both very positive signs that she would recover from her injuries. Unfortunately, that could not be said for the unfortunate GI.

Chapter Three

The Warden Meets the Giant

In my first year with the ADF&G, 1969, the wardens were not permitted to carry a defense weapon nor did we have off- the- road vehicles. This was a day that I sincerely wished that I had both. My assignment was to drive about 25 miles into the foot hills of the Chugach Range and patrol a fishery at Wolverine Lake. Nestled amongst the granite hills, lined with black birch trees the 500 acre gin-clear lake presented a fairy tale panorama.

The drive was a rather arduous one, especially when the vehicle du jour was a Ford station wagon designed to patrol the paved highways of Alaska. The road was sans gravel and was little more than a Cat trail cut through the permafrost. As spring approached   with its first faint warming rays of sunshine the trail turned into a quagmire in places. In short, the 25 mile trip took over 2 hours and the warden nearly ran out of expletives.

I was greeted at the lake by 50 or so eager anglers each driving a 4 wheel drive pickup truck, most having a small boat in the bed. I felt distinctly disadvantaged already and that was just a portent of events to come. Wolverine Lake was locally renowned for its share of 8 to 10 pound rainbow trout. They were highly prized considering that it takes about 10 years to grow a 10 pound rainbow in Alaska, the maximum growing season being only 4 months long. Since it was now early June, the really large spawning fish had made their way into the outlet stream to lay their eggs. It is at this time that they are particularly vulnerable to man and animal alike.

Soon after arriving I could hear a commotion coming from the stream. I cautiously but quickly made my way there. The sport fish biologists had done their job well by posting "no fishing" signs every 50 feet or so. Regardless, I soon spotted 6 or so young boys between the ages of 8 to 12 attempting to spear the fat rainbows with sharpened spruce branches. I yelled to stop yielded but yielded no result since on that day I was not in uniform. (after the muddy drive it was a good thing). After explaining that I was a fish and game officer and producing a badge they quickly complied. I then explained that to them that they were in a no fishing zone and were using illegal gear. After a brief sermon I escorted each boy to his respective parents. I told the parents that because of the boys' young age I would not be issuing citations but rather a written warning. Any subsequent violations would, however, result in a formal citation. All went well until the last boy.

As we arrived at the spot where the last boy's parents were camped I hollered a "Hello" and out of the camper/ trailer emerged a human being that resembled Goliath. The man was fully 6 feet 5 and weighed at least 350 pounds. I was not a small man either, 6 feet 3 and 200 pounds, but I was dwarfed by that behemoth. I had obviously awakened the bear from his nap and he was in a bad mood. To make things worse, I could smell alcohol oozing from his body. "Sir", I said, "Your son here has been spearing rainbows in the stream over there, and that is illegal." The next thing that I heard was a cascade of four letter words aimed at me followed by something to the effect that he was going to wring my #$%&*# neck.

Somehow I tended to believe in what he said. I soon found myself backing across the parking lot toward the lake while explaining to the man why he needed to cool down. That only seemed to further agitate him .He continued on his tirade telling me how worthless game wardens were and how much he hated them. In no time I was at the edge of the lake- it was either fight or flight. The former was not a good option unless I got real lucky and the latter would not look good on my resume.

This was a year before wardens were permitted to carry a side arm so I couldn't even try to frighten him a little with the "persuader." He continued to advance toward me with threats of drowning me and I started thinking of how my wife and child would survive without me. I decided that if he took one more step toward me I would have no choice but to rearrange his "Family Jewels". In his mid stride I suddenly heard a shrill female voice cry, "Harry, what the hell do you think you're doin'? How many times do I have to tell you that when you're drinkin'; stay in the camper! Now git!" Harry was helped along by a painful yank on his ear. The 5 foot 2, 125 pound rescuing angel apologized profusely for her husband's behavior and assured me that she would keep her son on a short leash. I started to believe that there must really be a God for He showed up that day.

Chapter Four

The Great Calf Moose Rescue

It was the first week of September, 1969, and I was entering into my 6th month with the state. I loved my job with a great zeal and hoped the honeymoon would never end. The city kids had just started back to school and the termination dust (sourdough talk for snow) had begun to powder the Chugach Mountain tops. In the lowlands it was still in the 50s.

I was scheduled for office duty that Indian summer day when the call came into the office that a calf moose was down in a local grade school yard. I pled for my supervisor to release me from the dreaded office duty and he reluctantly complied. Why spoil my honeymoon so soon? Within few minutes I was speeding on my way to the Mountain View area of town. I was met by an excited but apprehensive group of school kids who hurriedly showed me the location of the downed calf. After talking to one of the teachers I learned that a pack of dogs had been harassing the young moose and its mother for nearly an hour. Strangely, the mother was nowhere to be seen.

Perhaps she had led the pack away from her baby. The calf was lying, foam dripping from her lips, in an exhausted heap in a small grove of trees. In an effort to find some shelter from her assailants she instinctively chose the place. As I attempted to pick her up she tried desperately to rise but to no avail. I estimated her weight at about 100 pounds, fairly heavy for a moose born only 3 months earlier.

Her mother would wean her in a couple months so we would have to place the calf on a bottle for awhile. In another year she would weigh 400-450 pounds if no similar fate befell her. I carefully tied my patient's legs with ropes to somewhat contain her. I'd never done this kind of thing before. I was from Pennsylvania not Wyoming. I then placed her in the rear of the station wagon and waved good bye to the happy kids. I then headed south to the moose compound where the little one could be nursed back to health then released back to her natural habitat.

The afternoon traffic was unusually heavy downtown and after 20 minutes of crawling along the occupant in the rear became restless. I cast a wary eye in the rear view mirror and couldn't see anything but I could hear her struggling and thrashing around. There was no place to pull over so I decided to press on until I found a suitable pull off then I would check on my passenger. Suddenly, there was the clatter of hooves against the rear gate window, then the side door windows and before I knew it baby moose was in the front seat with me!

In an effort to drive the vehicle and protect myself from the sharp flying hooves I nearly wrecked. In desperation I threw a quick one- armed head lock on the moose which made steering nearly impossible. Just when it seemed as though I would pull off this herculean feat the moose made her move. The pain was absolutely agonizing as the long- legged creature placed a sharp hoof in my groin! I no longer pictured the moose as the victim but rather me. As I let loose of the animal and slumped over the wheel I turned on the emergency flashers and hoped for the best. Game warden down!

Almost immediately my door was flung open and I heard, "Are you all right"? I moaned a faint "I think so." I looked up into the weathered face of a man in a cowboy hat. He said that he had spotted me a ways back and figured that I was in trouble. He suggested that I stay put and he would take care of the "hooved - menace." He then did one of those rodeo things: He placed the rope in his teeth, grabbed the calf and threw her down, then wrapped her up like a Christmas present in 5 seconds flat. If I was able I would have cheered. I thanked him and he said something like, "Take 'er easy pardner, lucky I was behind ya." Yes, lucky…or was I blessed?

Chapter Five

Scar Head and the Sea Lions

When I was in one of my private teenage escape times reading Outdoor Life or Field and Stream I came across an article about some characters in Alaska that mesmerized me for days. The true story was about an Alaskan big game guide and his three sons. The story held me spell bound because they didn't seem to belong in this century. These four could well have lived in the days of Boone, Carson, or Crockett. Perhaps that is why these peculiar men chose to live in what has come to be known as the Last Frontier- Alaska.

I will refrain from using their real names for fear that they may still be living and come looking for me. However, the similarity between the names is real. The father's name was Joe, the eldest son was named Joe Jr., the next was Joey, and the youngest was Joey John. All the boys called the father, Sir. According to the magazine story Joe Sr. took the eldest son along with him to help guide some clients on a grizzly hunt. Joe literally hunted in his back yard, i.e. the Talkeetna Mountains.

When the hunters arrived at Joe's to hunt for bear, moose, caribou, or the elusive Dall sheep he quickly placed them on horseback and within minutes they were in prime hunting country. The Chickaloon River knifed its way through the heart of the mountains to meet the mighty Matanuska not far from the guide's homestead. The backdrop was truly magnificent drawing hunters and photographers from around the world. Joe was totally unaffected by protocol and the social pecking order.

His clients all ate 'C' rations no matter who they were, ambassadors or troubadours. Joe's reply to complainers was the same, "If you don't like the food you can go hungry!" Many a once- pampered client was humbled after a week or so with Joe. For the snooty ones who felt offended and demanded that he return them to civilization, he would retort, "you can leave any time but you gotta walk out." No one took him up on it.

Something went very wrong on this bear hunt. If my memory serves me correctly, one of the hunters, a novice from Europe, shot a fair sized grizzly in a non vital spot on its body. This was the guide's worst nightmare since he then was duty bound to track the wounded bear down alone so as not to unduly endanger the client. As the story went, Joe and Joe Jr. followed the bloody trail directly into the thick brush. The huge animal was waiting for them and Jr. was mauled by the animal. Fortunately, the wounds were not life threatening but limited to severe bite wounds to the head. The magazine later showed current photos of the young man revealing what appeared to be deep scars running the length of his skull. These were scars that he would carry for the rest of his life.

"Huba, I want you to check out this complaint out with the Troopers." These were the orders of the day from my direct supervisor, Bill Martin, Senior Protection Officer. Bill was a native of Washington State, part American Indian, and a solid 260 pounds. He had about 5 years in the business at the time and quickly won my admiration for his savvy. The complaint was scribbled on a piece of note paper and briefly stated that Joe Sr. was a suspect in a homicide at the tiny village of Chickaloon, about 50 miles east of Anchorage along the Glenn Highway. I quickly jumped into my station wagon and headed for the nearest Trooper dispatch station in Palmer. The assigned trooper then started to unveil the details:

It seemed as though there was a dispute near Joe's homestead in Chickaloon. Allegedly Joe's neighbor was beating his own son while in a drunken rage and had been warned by Joe on repeated occasions. The neighbor didn't heed Joe's warnings so Joe methodically trudged through the deep snow, rifle in hand, to pay a visit. Joe knocked on the cabin door and when the man opened the door he was greeted by the muzzle blast of a 30-06. Apparently Joe let his rifle have the last word.

After a somewhat cursory investigation, the troopers determined to charge the murderer with 2nd degree manslaughter which was eventually reduced to careless use of a firearm. This was not a highly unusual charge. It was said in those days that a man would get a lesser charge for shooting his wife than for shooting a moose out of season. In fact the term "Spenard divorce" (Spenard is a suburb of Anchorage) was a rather common label for a domestic shooting that took place during the long dark Alaskan winter. It seemed as though folks would contract "cabin fever" from being cooped up during that season. The strange malady often seemed to be an ample defense against a murder charge.

My involvement in the case was to help determine whether Joe's crime was sufficient to be considered one involving "moral turpitude." If it was Joe would lose his state hunting guide's license. After weeks of haggling the department decided to suspend Joe's license for a year. That fall there were many reports of old Joe guiding hunters but each time he was investigated he would simply reply "my boys were guiding, I was only along for the ride." The last time I heard, he was 85 and moving a little slower, but still feeding his clients "C" rations in the high Talkeetnas.

Perhaps three weeks later I received a request from the District Supervisor, Don Tetzlaff to check on an alleged illegal sale of sea otter hides. Don was the senior on staff with 12 years experience. He was originally from Michigan and we had hunting Dall sheep in common. At the time I had a sheep in the Boone and Crockett Record Book which won me much respect with Don. He suggested that I go "undercover" since that would be the most effective way to crack this case.

I had never, still being a rookie, done any undercover work but was assured by my superiors that the only way to learn the ropes was to make good plans then just do it. My first step was to talk to all the local taxidermists to see if I could pick up any leads. This yielded no leads. A few days later Tetzlaff called me and told me he had a firm lead on who the culprit may be – none other than Joe Jr. from Chickaloon ! This made things a lot easier and I started checking the local bars to see if I could locate him. I didn't find Joe but I did locate someone who knew where he lived. I was posing as a fur buyer so as not to appear suspicious. Within a few hours I was poised at the door of a rundown cabin located near downtown Anchorage. I nervously knocked on the rustic wooden door and waited while a voice sounded from inside "hold on a minute". I got the idea that I was being checked out from a secret vantage point to determine who I was.

I must have looked the part of a fur buyer for the door soon squeaked open and the short inhabitant said, "Yah, can I help ya?" I replied that my name was Al and was a fur buyer. Surprisingly he motioned me in. "Wanna coffee?' "Sure, thanks, I replied." We sat and as my eyes became accustomed to the dimly lit room I started to make out the features of this Alaskan mountain man. He was small and wiry – maybe 5 ft.8 and 150 lbs. He appeared to have lived about 40 very hard years and his thin greasy grayish blond hair was pulled back into a make shift pony tail.

The blended smell of cigarettes and booze seemed to be part of his body. There was something strange, however, about the irregular way that his hair had grown. I shifted in my chair and squinted to get a clearer view but couldn't. I then made an excuse to stand and nonchalantly moved closer. Yes, now I could see it clearly: multiple deep scars running from the front of his scalp toward the rear. My mind kicked into rewind.

It was him! The eldest son of the grizzly guide from Outdoor Life magazine; the one who was mauled 20 years earlier! I must admit that I was so awestruck that I had to reseat myself. After a few deep breaths and a gulp of coffee I remembered why I was there.

"Say Joe, do you have any furs for sale"? I blurted. "What kind" he said. I related that I specialized in fine furs: wolverine, marten, and wolf, trying to bait him in to see if he might have some sea otter hides. Intuitively I knew that I had gained some degree of trust albeit it slight and perhaps fleeting. He said that he only had sea lion hides for sale at the time. I asked if I could see them and he agreed.

He took me to a metal trailer to the rear of the cabin and threw open the doors. To my amazement there were nearly 200 hides inside, all legal. The informant had obviously mistaken sea lions for sea otters. The sea otter had been protected by federal law for decades having been hunted to near extinction for its highly prized fur. After a few cursory questions I offered that I wasn't interested in the sea lions and thanked him for his time. What a memory : a man scarred inwardly and outwardly, perhaps born out of synch with time doing his best to scratch out a living in very harsh environment. God bless you Joe Jr.

Chapter Six

Metro Moose

As the winter snow seasonally creeps its way down the slopes of the Chugach Mountains the residents of Anchorage prepare themselves for winter sports: cross country skiing, snow mobiling, ice skating, sled riding, downhill skiing and snow shoeing. There is no way to prepare, however, for the most dangerous of all winter sports – moose dodging. Each winter dozens of city dwellers are injured, some seriously and even fatally by the moose who invade the city to avoid the deep snows of the higher elevations. The number of moose/ auto collisions increases dramatically as well as more personal encounters; which brings to mind one particular incident from the winter of 1970.

I was greeted as I entered the office one morning with, "OK, Huba, it's your turn to help the biologists. They are having big trouble with a mother moose downtown." With my usual adrenaline rush I leaped into the familiar green station wagon and quickly accelerated toward downtown. The scene wasn't hard to spot for a small crowd had gathered outside a fenced-in snow covered parking lot. Inside was a rather large female moose with her yearling calf close by her side. She had marked out her territory and was not allowing any cars into the lot.

The lot was gated but someone had either left the gate open during the night or soon after the gate was opened in the morning mother moose and calf strolled into the lot. The game biologists who were first on the scene tried shooing the moose off with yells and then fire crackers to no avail. They decided that the situation called for more serious measures so why not call on the rookie game warden? It would be a good place to test his metal.

After assessing the situation I reluctantly decided to enter moose's arena. I cautiously stepped through the gate and saw the moose, a mere fifty feet away, eyes fixed on me and her ears nervously twitching from side to side. A moose's eyes are the poorest of their senses but their large ears and nose are keen sensors. My aim was to somehow force her out the gate on the far side of the lot. To make matters more interesting, in my haste to reach the scene, I had left my boots at the office and was now wearing my slick soled office dress shoes. As I gingerly walked toward her the hackles on her back immediately stood up and she mounted a warning charge which covered about twenty feet. That was enough to send me scurrying behind one of the few vehicles in the lot.

Now standing only thirty feet away I was in a position to fully appreciate her size: approximately six feet at the shoulder and weighing between 900 and 1000 pounds; not a huge moose by Alaskan standards but big enough to easily kill me. The strength and killing power of a moose is grossly under estimated. Their sharp hooves have been known to kill a mature grizzly bear by striking them in the chest. I fought hard to keep those thoughts out of my mind. Another attempt to advance toward her with the hope of herding her out the gate was met with a more serious charge. This one sent me sprawling, placing a truck between me and the very angry moose. I had just narrowly missed being kicked with her lethal cloven weapons. It was at this point that a cooler head would have to prevail. After composing myself and waiting for the laughter of the onlookers to subside I took a more sane approach. I proceeded to clear everyone away from the fence and ordered them across the street. I then placed the biologists at the entry ways to keep vehicles from trying to enter the lot while I sat in my vehicle across the street. We all then waited for nature to take its course. Within 15 minutes the moose felt unthreatened and nonchalantly trotted out the gate into a nearby wooded area with her calf close behind her .The lesson learned? Never force the issue with a female and a kid, moose or otherwise.

Chapter Seven

Hole in the Wall Polar Bears

W hile still a rookie I can recall many "snafus" on my part, one of the most memorable is the following: In the winter of 1969 while working out of the Anchorage office I received an anonymous call from McGrath (250 miles northwest of Anchorage) reporting that an illegal shipment of polar bear hides was being flown to Anchorage via a Cessna 185 on skis. The logical place to land was Lake Hood which was frozen at that time of year. I quickly drove my department vehicle there and parked at a suitable vantage point.

A half hour later I spotted a south bound 185 approaching the lake for a landing. Using my binoculars I later spotted the pilot and his passenger unload three canvas bags then stand near the plane. A few minutes later a pick up arrived to receive the men and their contraband. I followed them at a safe distance to a nearby building which housed a flight service operation and observed them take the canvas bags through the front door. Bingo! Caught them red-handed, or so I thought.

I called dispatch on my radio and asked for a backup while I went to the local judge to obtain a search warrant based on the established "probable cause." (probable cause is the legal term for reasons or grounds for searching a vehicle or dwelling.)

Minutes later Officer Brown, another rookie 9 months my junior arrived on the scene. I quickly briefed him stressing the point to not let the men and the bear hides leave the building. Nodding his head he affirmed that he would handle it.

Judge Jones in Anchorage, being a strong advocate for the ADF&G, without delay issued the search warrant even though it was his day off. With warrant in hand I drove swiftly back to Lake Hood. Officer Brown proudly advised me that all was well and that the men and bears were still inside the building. I then proceeded to the building with my partner following close behind. After entering the office I asked to see the owner or person in charge and summarily presented the search warrant to him. His reaction surprised me for he calmly said, "no problem." We then proceeded to the warehouse in the rear of the building fully expecting to find the three canvas bags. Instead we found a gaping 4 foot hole in outer wall of the building! Surprised and embarrassed I found sarcasm to be my only immediate relief.

"Oh, I see that you are renovating your building!" Smiling victoriously he simply said, "Yes we are." I then informed the man that he had indeed pulled one over on us, but that the ADF&G would not take it lightly and that his flight service would be on our "bad guy list" which would prove to be a real nuisance for him. Obviously what had happened was that after leaving Brown to oversee the operation the violators chopped a hole in the wall, loaded the bears in a vehicle and made the getaway. Interestingly, the flight service pick up had never moved. Another vehicle had been used but how would I ever find it? I didn't have the heart to chew out the rookie for allowing the escape for I was just as culpable for not instructing him to watch the rear of the building.

Somewhere I had read that many times a criminal will return to the scene of the crime. Would he possibly by some chance return to Lake Hood? After dark that night I drove out there and parked a hundred feet or so away from the crime scene and waited.... and waited. This was the part of my job that I didn't like even though it was an important part of it. On this bitter cold winter night I would have much rather been downing a few Coors at Chilkoot Charlies. As I was nodding off I was startled by headlights coming my way. The vehicle slowly turned behind the building and stopped for a few long seconds then proceeded to slowly pull away. I quickly pulled my vehicle behind his and then I noticed the compelling evidence on the trunk lid- white hand prints! Tell tale prints from the curing salt used on the bear hides! I then put on my red flashers, pulled the vehicle over and ordered the driver to open the trunk.

He nervously complied. In the trunk I found ample quantities of salt, polar bear hair but no bear hides. I had discovered another accomplice but without possession of the hides there was little that I could do except warn and advise him. After running an ID check on him I discovered that he was the chief shipping agent for a major airline. The department had been working for months trying to determine how illegal wildlife goods were being shipped out of the state. Could this be the source? I was learning that even snafus could lead to something profitable. The suspect was asked to come into the ADF&G office a few days later.

As the man was being interrogated he became as nervous as a cat in a roomful of rocking chairs. I had indeed found one of the chief operators in the shipping of wildlife contraband. A visit to the airline's warehouse yielded thousands of dollars of contraband ivory and other wildlife parts. The illegal operation had in effect been shut down. Meanwhile the rookie had learned another valuable lesson on how to turn a stumbling stone into a building block.

Part Two

The Rookie Leaves Home

Chapter One

Polar Bears at Point Hope

My lungs were on fire and the fronts of my legs were numb from the effects of the minus 40 degree cold. I could feel the strength slowly ebbing out of my body. I had to find shelter soon or my flickering life as a game warden would soon be snuffed out. I stumbled on shouldering my 75 pound duffle bag, fighting for breath and trying to focus on the trail in front of me. Someone had messed up big time; why was there no one to pick me up at the airstrip? I would have to deal with that later. At last, several hundred yards away I spotted a wisp of smoke which meant a dwelling of some kind. I gathered all my remaining power and tried to quicken the pace.

At long last I arrived at the source of the smoke - an underground lodging. I hurried down a tunnel which I hoped would lead to the interior. After a hunched over course of 20 feet or so I came to a crude wooden door which I desperately flung open. The heat from inside hit me like a blast furnace but it felt good. The glasses I was wearing fogged up immediately so I could see nothing except some blurry bright lights around me. The roar of laughter brought me quickly to my senses. I hurriedly cleaned my glasses and noticed that the small 20x20 roomed was filled with Native people staring at me and laughing.

I had stumbled into the town's only café! I honestly couldn't blame them for laughing. What a sight I must have been, an officer of the law representing the honorable ADF&G dressed like a "city slicker" in street shoes, a light jacket, no hat, and no gloves. I took the subsequent ribbing good naturedly and soon won their favor by being friendly and approachable. After depositing my gear in a back room I was invited to share some coffee with a few of the locals. The Eskimos are not ones to ask a lot of personal questions and were overall on the quiet side. That being the case, I proffered a few general inquiries of my own, concerning the weather, how plentiful the bears were, when whaling season began, what they did for fun during the long winters, etc. After they determined that I was genuinely interested in their culture, the discussion began to flow freely and they volunteered interesting bits of information regarding their way of life.

Over the next several weeks I would learn much more about the Inupiat Eskimo way of life. Inupiat literally means "real people." As I got to know these wonderful people better they really did become to me just that - real. The big ice breaker came later in the evening when I was challenged to shoot pool with them. Although I was an accomplished shooter, I was no match for these Point Hope sharks. They knew how to read the table perfectly, with all of its warps, dips, and slants - I did not. I used that as an excuse for every defeat and they simply laughed and rubbed it in at every opportunity. As the weeks passed, however, I did learn to hold my own but still was no match for their best shooters.

After a year of acting as a game warden, those in power deemed me worthy of a task that would certainly stretch my abilities. The ADF&G had a way of "quick seasoning" their boys, however, sometimes the process resulted in "burn out". A normal work week during hunting season would entail about 100 plus hours. We were paid for 37 1/2 hours which translated to our really loving our work. Going in we all knew we weren't in it for the money. My lot had been drawn in the spring of 1971 to help monitor the polar bear hunts at Point Hope which was situated on the Bering Sea approximately 1000 miles to the northwest of Anchorage and a scant 60 miles from the Russian island of Big Diomede.

Point Hope had been the headquarters for polar bear hunters from the four corners of the earth for over 30 years. During early spring big game guides with their well -healed hunters would congregate on a stretch of frozen seashore from Nome to Point Hope a distance of about 200 miles. Their goal was to bag one of the most prized big game animals in the world - the great white Polar Bear. This bear is the largest of the land carnivores, reaching a standing height of 11 feet and weighing in at nearly 2000 pounds. Their diet consists mainly of seals although in summer they will forage for plant life ashore.

Despite their intimidating proportions they are surprisingly docile. They like their neighbor, the wolf, have been the victim of many myths concerning their vicious nature. In my research of these animals I would be hard pressed to find a single incident of an unprovoked attack by a wolf and only a few isolated incidents concerning the polar bear. In all of these cases the bear has undoubtedly viewed the human as part of his food chain as they trespassed into its domain.

A New Sheriff in Town

Just prior to arriving at Point Hope I had the dubious pleasure of spending a few days 90 miles to the south in Kotzebue. I was to wait there until the logistics were in place for the month long monitoring program. My temporary domicile was a gray weather beaten place on the beach called "Tony's Old Oar House" (seriously). It was owned by a burly Italian fellow who migrated from New York City a few years prior. He prided himself by having a cuisine that would rival that of any big city. Fresh meat and vegetables were flown in daily. My favorite was the center cut pork chops, a full 2 inches thick and never frozen (to keep anything from freezing is a mean feat in the Arctic).

It was also a gathering place for the bear guides to stock up on supplies and meet with their clients. Since this was my first trip to the Arctic there was much that I did not know. The first was not being aware of the "bad blood" that existed between the guides and the wardens.

While seated at the bar ordering breakfast on my first morning the waiter remarked "you sure are brave". When asked what that meant he replied that the wardens never eat where the guides do because it causes trouble. I asked him if that was an invitation to leave and he quickly retorted, "No, but you'll have to take your chances." I casually ate my breakfast without incident, however, I did get a few dirty looks from a guide or two. Word quickly got out that a game warden had dared violate one of the guides' rules. The atmosphere at dinner changed dramatically, especially when the drinks started flowing.

As I sat alone at a table savoring my center cut pork chops the stares grew more intense and soon remarks were circulating around the room. The remarks turned into threats and I began to feel a little uncomfortable. As I saw it, the reputation of the ADF&G was on the line and I refused to be intimidated. At one point a rather large native assistant guide goaded by his boss approached my table and told me that I'd better leave or else. Feeling a bit like Matt Dillon at the Long Branch Saloon I decided to call his challenge.

I stood up and informed him that if anyone was going to leave it was going to be him and that I didn't appreciate having my dinner disturbed. My 6 foot 3 frame carrying a weight trained frame was enough to discourage him and he walked away muttering. I knew, however, that this was only a temporary situation for I was hopelessly out numbered and my antagonists were growing braver with each drink.

This was clearly a case where my zeal and bravado had exceeded my wisdom. As I was pondering my plight I was approached by a diminutive native man who identified himself as an ADF&G coworker. He informed me that he'd been in this position before and the smart thing to do would be to leave immediately and worry about our reputation later. It made perfect sense to me. The next day in my fervor to leave and get on the job I rushed out of my toasty digs into a warm plane and never thought about donning warm clothes. That accounted for my chilly arrival in Point Hope.

It took me an hour or so to recover from my cold reception at Point Hope. The fronts of my thighs were mildly frost bitten and my lungs were frosted as well. After a couple of cups of strong native coffee I felt refreshed. The Eskimos were friendly but naturally reserved. It had been a while since they had seen a warden and didn't know what to expect. For the most part they felt that the wardens were intruding on their inherent subsistence rights by enforcing the Alaskan Game laws.

In many areas they were free to break the laws simply because they were native Alaskans and felt that the law didn't apply to them. Part of my reason for being there was not only to enforce the law but to educate them as to what the laws were since many were illiterate. My most serious concerns were not with the natives, many of which were ignorant of the laws, but with the bear guides who not only flagrantly broke the laws but flaunted their ability to do so.

I spent the night in a cramped room attached to the café and was awakened the next morning by the roar of snow mobiles outside. My task that day would to procure a place to stay for the next month. By word of mouth (no phone service in those days) I learned that a lady by the name of Tilly had reserved a small house for me. A resident soon pointed the house out to me and I began to ready it for habitation since it had been uninhabited for some time. The first thing to do was to get some heat in the house since it was more than minus 40 degrees below zero outdoors, counting the chill factor, and only slightly warmer inside where there was no wind. Fortunately there was enough fuel in the oil barrel to fire up the antiquated stove.

As I waited for the house to warm I busied myself with locating the ADG&G bear biologist so as to coordinate my work with his. That task was to measure each bear hide after being skinned and fleshed then take skull measurements and gather other biological data. All this was necessary to properly manage a species which was on the brink of being an endangered species. My job was to make sure that the bears were legally taken, properly tagged and hunters and guides thoroughly examined for proper licensure etc. Most of this work was done in the home of a professional skinner where the hunters would first bring their trophies for care.

Management of this species was a two pronged cooperative effort between the biologists and the protection department that I worked for. My theory was that studies of the bear were necessary for the long term health of the bears but we were in such a position that something very proactive had to be done to save the species. It was my opinion as well as that of more experienced game officials that the bear kill each year exceeded the safe limits of a sustained yield. To put it simply, too many bears were being killed each year and many more were not being reported since they were being taken illegally, either out of season or the legal bag limit was being violated.

My passion was to do all humanly possible to ensure that the bears were taken legally and that each hunter and guide took only their legal limit and no more. It was a simple equation for me: the fewer bears you kill the more bears you will have left to reproduce the following year therefore the numbers will naturally increase. Someone in Washington agreed with me for in 1972 the Federal Marine Mammals Act was passed which banned the hunting of many sea mammals including the polar bear which could only be hunted by Alaskan Natives. The polar bears quickly recovered and are no longer an endangered species. The polar bear guides did not fare as well.

Tilly's House

After finishing my day's work I went to check on my new home, Tilly's house. I was surprised to discover that despite having the oil stove running at full heat for 12 hours the temperature in the house had only risen to 0. I decided that that was a little too chilly to live in so I would let the heat run for another 12 hours and check back the following day. Upon returning I found the temperature had only risen a couple of degrees. I would have to find another solution. One of the locals informed me that I was losing most of the heat through the floor since the house was not built on the ground but was elevated on 3 foot pilings.

A snow block wall built around the base of the house might work. Since the days were short at that time of the year, with sunset at 4pm, I had to work quickly. I borrowed a snow knife which resembled a machete and started to cut blocks of compacted snow into 2 by 2 by 1 foot chunks. It was my first try at building a snow house but I felt like a kid again and the project was completed before sundown. I returned the next morning and found the house to be a toasty 40 degrees which over the course of a few days rose to a nearly comfortable 50 degrees. With my Eddie Bauer Arctic sleeping bag and Woolrich clothing I would fare well in my new home.

Don't Drink the Yellow Water

Finding potable water in the Arctic can pose a significant problem especially during the winter season. There are virtually no running streams and no deep wells so the sources for water are limited. When I asked my Eskimo neighbors where to get water they advised me to purchase some ice from the vendors who were easy to locate. After putting out the word that I needed ice for water several vendors came to my door. The prices for a sled load of ice ranged from 10 to 25 dollars. Being a frugal person I chose the 10 dollar load sold by a teenager. Since I had no water at all I encouraged him to rush the delivery which he agreed to. An hour later he arrived with the valuable cargo.

I hurriedly chipped off pieces and placed them in a pot on top of the oil stove. This would be my sole means for drinking and bathing. Being both thirsty and smelly I anxiously waited for the ice to melt. Watching the ice melt quickly turned into a shocking experience. The water was yellow and there was a mass of dog hairs floating on the top! I learned why there was 10 dollar and 25 dollar ice.

The 10 dollar stuff was cut from a pond right in town and the 25 dollar ice was cut from a pond located miles away from town and the dogs. I immediately summoned the vendor of the 25 buck ice and ordered a load advising him that it better be clean. He assured me that it would be. For the next month my routine for cooking, drinking and bathing was to break off a chunk of ice melt it and use it. I soon forgot about the luxury of running water and a flush toilet - which brings to mind another story.

Eskimo Entertainers

Each evening between 6 and 7 I was treated by visit from several young Eskimo boys ranging in age from 9 to 12 years. They delighted in showing off their tumbling skills and other physical tricks. This would go on initially for hours but because of my work schedule I had to impose some limits. Their gymnastic skills were truly amazing and I wondered how they could develop if they had professional training. I always rewarded them for their efforts with some Hershey bars. The candy, however, was not the motivator for the kids it was just the shear enjoyment they received from performing for an appreciative stranger.

The kids soon started arriving earlier in the day to see if they could help out with the chores. I agreed to hire them to sweep the floors, wash dishes and other tasks. The one chore that was the nastiest but paid the most (1dollar) was emptying the "honey bucket". For the unenlightened reader it was simply a 5 gallon bucket with a crude toilet seat fasted to it.

Depending on how many visitors I had the bucket needed emptying about twice a week. The designated bucket boy arrived one evening for his initial dump. It was a particularly windy evening with the chill factor at minus 60 degrees. The procedure for dumping the bucket was to carry it to the street and locate the 55 gallon drum placed there for that purpose and pour the contents into it.

When the drums were full they were then transported by sled to a lake where they remained until the spring thaw. When the ice melted the drums sank out of sight and that completed the "sewage disposal cycle of the far North". The kid went out the door with his load and seemed to handle it well considering it probably weighed 30 pounds or so. After 10 minutes or so I became concerned about the boy not returning. I peeked out the door to see if I could spot him. I heard him whimpering at the side of the house and quickly coaxed him inside. What a mess my eyes were now beholding!

The poor kid was covered from head to toe with "honey". I got him to take off the soiled clothes and I started to melt some ice for bath water. After helping him bathe I gave him a fresh change of my clothes. My being 6 feet 3 and him about 4 feet 3 didn't make much difference now. I sent him out the door with a smile on his face and a bonus in his pocket. My young apprentice had learned a valuable lesson: when dumping the "honey bucket" always stand upwind.

Brothers and a Bribe

About two weeks into my stay at Pt. Hope I received a dinner invitation from an infamous bear guide. I felt suspicious and honored at the same time since his hunting client was one of two brothers from the Indianapolis 500 Club, both men having won the race. I reluctantly accepted the invitation although I "smelled a rat." I soon found myself seated across a makeshift plank table from one man whom I had seen on TV sports and the other a notorious big game guide known throughout Alaska. My normally cool composure was evaporating as beads of sweat ran down the back of my neck. I don't remember much about the meal except it was very good considering the primitive conditions.

I do, however, remember the drinks that flowed freely after the dinner. I graciously but cautiously accepted each drink intuitively knowing that there was an agenda brewing. I slowed down on the drinking while the others became intoxicated. The client proceeded to tell me how his older brother, on a recent hunt had shot a polar bear larger than his; his being a 9 footer and his brother's a 10 footer. I congratulated him on his trophy but he brushed it off announcing that he wanted to shoot a bigger one than his brother. I informed him that he would have to wait another 3 years to do that since the bag limit for polar bears was one every 3 years. He then presented me with a sterling silver cigarette lighter beautifully engraved with his name and the year that he won the Indy 500.

I attempted to give it back several times but he insisted that it was a gift. Against my better judgment I kept it. He then again asked if he could shoot another bear while he was reaching for his wallet. I then informed him that it was a serious offense to bribe a law officer. He then backed off and I was glad that I hadn't had a few more drinks or I might have stupidly taken the bribe. While I was there I asked the guide to show me his guide's license. He then coyly produced last year's license. The ruse was now fully exposed. When I told the guide that he was in violation of the law and that on the morrow I would be issuing him a citation he became very angry. To avoid an ugly scene I decided to exit the lodge and thanked him for the meal and the drinks.

As I closed the door behind me and sighed with relief, I was greeted by a blast of minus 40 degree air that served to partially sober me up. However, as I proceeded to trudge through the drifting snow I soon realized that the drinks had taken their toll on me – I was noticeably disoriented. The only light was that of the aurora borealis which thankfully was bright enough to help me make out the shape of the Inupiat houses partially hidden under the snow drifts.

My previous trail to the guide's camp was drifted over making it impossible to retrace my tracks back to Tilly's house. The houses were situated about 50 yards apart and the streets were buried beneath several feet of packed snow making difficult to locate my house. As I stumbled on I became worried as all the houses started to look the same to me. Since the hour was late, about one AM, the houses were unlit which further hampered my navigation. My next step was an exciting one: There was a snarl, the snapping of teeth and a flurry of powdery snow as I had stepped on a sled dog that was buried under the drifting snow. He was soon joined by a dozen of his partners as they emerged from their frigid beds barking and snarling creating a cacophony of sounds that served to clear more of the alcohol fog from my head. Luckily the dogs were docile, as most sled dogs are, and were probably as startled as I was.

The commotion elicited a cabin light to come on and as the resident peered out his doorway I recognized him as my next door neighbor! If I hadn't stepped on that dog I might have become a fatality as some do that drink too much and wander around in a drunken stupor. It isn't unusual to find missing persons each spring as the snow melts and reveals the victims. I was thankful to stumble through the doorway into the relative comfort of my "warm" 45 degree house.

Wearily I crawled into my cozy sleeping bag as the thoughts of the day danced through my mind. My bliss was not to last long for I soon heard a loud thump at the door. I soon discovered drunken man who literally fell in as I opened the door. I helped him onto the couch and he was soon fast asleep. Someone was watching over us on that bitterly cold Arctic night.

Chapter Two

The Academy

The fall of 1970 was highlighted by my entering the State Trooper Academy in picturesque Sitka, Alaska. Although I had served with the department for 18 months, it was mandatory, at some point, that all state law enforcement personnel attend the academy - "boot camp for cops". The setting was idyllic. Situated on the southern Alaskan Panhandle in the midst of America's northernmost rain forest, the area enjoys moderate temperatures ranging on the average of 65 degrees in July to the 30's in January. The surrounding cold Pacific waters abound with 5 species of salmon, giant halibut, king crab, and shrimp. A perfect fare for perpetually hungry "trooper candidates."

The academy itself was located on the grounds of the venerated Sheldon Jackson College which was founded in 1878 by the Presbyterian Church as an Alaskan Native training school. Native students at my time comprised about 30% of the enrollment. Although the facilities were aged they were very well kept and comfortable and the food was more than adequate.

Most of the classes were rather boring except for firearm training, high speed pursuit driving and physical training. It seemed as though these 3 classes were specifically designed just for me: I loved firearms of any kind, inherited from my father, driving fast was not inherited but definitely learned as a teenager who possessed a "lead foot"; and I was part owner of a gym in downtown Anchorage so weight training was a big part of my life.

All of our training involved competing against our fellow trainees. I remember placing near the top on the pistol range, beat out by a seasoned former California Highway Patrolman. It was quite an honor to train beside someone who was a former member of CHPS (California Highway Patrol). We had 4 ex CHPS men with us. They all left California the year before and relocated in Alaska. All had been either directly or indirectly involved in the ambush of a dozen or so California Patrolmen leaving many dead or wounded. I was serving with heroes and felt very honored.

I thought that I was "hot stuff" when it came to the high speed pursuit driving. I was quickly humbled. My early days of driving stock street cars did me no good on this course. The vehicle of choice was a super- charged Chevy 409 and was downright scary! The pursuit course was set up on an abandoned airstrip just outside the city beside the water. It was 1/2 mile figure 8 course laid out with pylons. The idea was to get through the course as quickly as possible while being timed by the attending instructor. He was an interesting individual to say the least.

He was a Trooper who was placed on special duty due to injuries suffered in a high speed chase a few years earlier.

Sergeant K, as we called him, walked with a noticeable limp but it didn't hamper his ability to teach us how to drive "the Trooper way". I did my best on the course and was placed in the upper fourth of the class. The champion was "Pete," an old game warden from Wisconsin who had attended a previous academy or two. There was one formal competition left, the pentathlon. The challengers would be formidable but I was confident that I would win. The events consisted of sit-ups, push- ups, chin- ups, the standing broad jump and the mile run. We had 8 weeks to train so all men would be well prepared. My training partner was my roommate, a short, wiry city policeman from the state capitol, Juneau. Doug was a former high school track star who could run and jump well but was woeful in his performances in the other 3 events. I liked Doug so I decided to coach him. He learned quickly and his progress was rapid.

The big day of the final pentathlon competition came just a few days before the class graduation. In the first event, I did 68 sit-ups in 60 seconds (an academy record) and had no one close to me. Push-ups were next and I managed 65 in 60 seconds, another record and again no one close. Chins were next and I did 15, one better than my closest competitor. Now it got a little tougher- the standing broad jump. I knew going in that with two sore knees (old sports injuries) jumping and running would be tough but I would be a trooper (pun intended). Wrapping the knees helped and I succeeded in a leap of 11 feet plus only to be out done by two other guys by a matter of a few inches.

Next came the big test, the mile run. By now my knees were screaming for mercy but there would be none given. I rewrapped and took off on the run. I finished in about 6 minutes, a respectable time, but eclipsed by my roommate's time of 5 minutes plus! Now we waited for the final point tally. Well, shockingly, I lost by a couple of points. The run did me in. I congratulated the winner….. Doug, my roommate! I never did let him forget that I was his coach and we must share the victory. Being my buddy, he agreed to that but of course kept the trophy.

What a wonderful couple of months those were. I met some men who still occupy a special place in my heart and mind. One was Pat Sheeley. He was a former Oregon State trooper who was assigned to keep the law and order in the logging camps of the coastal area. Pat was young, in his early thirties, 6 feet tall and a muscular 240 pounds. On one of our "off "evenings we were all swapping tales and Pat proceeded to brag about numerous occasions when he and his team would virtually bring quick order to a rowdy and drunken logging camp. Pat said he still had the lumps and scars to remind him of those days.

When it came around to me I was still a rookie and didn't have much to say regarding my law enforcement exploits but there were many "extracurricular" tales that brought laughs and jeers from my classmates. Because of our overinflated egos we all knew that sooner or later Sheeley and Huba would have to face off to see who the strongest trooper was. Since Pat and I genuinely liked each other we agreed that a boxing or wrestling match was not a consideration for fear of hurting each other. Pat suggested something that he was sure he could beat me at - arm wrestling, for he was undefeated.

I reluctantly consented. I had arm wrestled some but my record was not unblemished for I had competed against some real animals from the gym in Anchorage. So Pat and I squared off one evening and the bets were down and he was understandably the heavy favorite. We took our positions, locked grips (he had the grip of a gorilla) and waited for the referee's command to go. From the start Sheeley gave it all he had to catch me off guard, but surprisingly I held my own which badly shook his confidence. Slowly but steadily I wore him down and then slammed his arm to the table. That took all of about one minute. The room was dead silent, then, Sheeley, catching his breath, offered, "best of three!" With my confidence bolstered I quickly agreed. The next match lasted just seconds and it was a repeat of the first.

I was surprised at the ease of the contest and learned that Pat was probably the stronger but had little endurance. He never needed it for being so strong he was used to ending things quickly. Pat was surely embarrassed but our mutual respect for each other was cemented that day. A few days later we all left our training grounds for our respective posts spread over the State. Sadly most of us rarely saw each other again, but when we did we shared a lot fond memories of the State Trooper Academy.

Chapter Three

The Deadliest Catch

The fall and winter of 1969 found the novice warden deeply entrenched in his new challenge, the King Crab fishery on the Bering Sea. Nowadays nearly everyone who watches TV is familiar with the hit series, "The Deadliest Catch." My job was to make sure the commercial crab boats were licensed as well as the crew members. In addition I was responsible to make sure the boats were not fishing in closed waters and that the fishing only took place during the strictly regulated seasons and hours. Only mature crabs could be taken so random checks had to be made. At this time a measurement of the crab's carapace was taken.

The carapace is the shell containing the crustacean's organs otherwise known as the body of the crab. In most cases the size of the carapace was an indicator of the age of the crab; the larger the shell, the older the crab. At that time the minimum legal size was 8 inches. It was not unusual, however, to measure shells exceeding 12 inches or more.

The King Crab is the largest crab in the world with measurements from claw tip to tip at times exceeding 6 feet. That, of course was in the late 60's and early 70's. Today, due to heavy harvesting, a 4 footer would be a large one. The King Crab still ranks among the true seafood delicacies known around the world. Although found throughout most of the North Pacific, the cold pristine waters of the Bering Sea, are by far its favorite haunt. Although fished to the point of depletion in the late 70's, strict harvest regulations are now insuring a safe sustained yield.

Due to a lack of available personnel I was sent solo to the fishing headquarters of Dutch Harbor to assume my duties. Dutch Harbor, known as "Dutch", was the headquarters of the U.S. North Pacific Naval Fleet in WWII. In June of 1942 it was the scene of two aerial attacks by the Japanese Fleet. The damage inflicted by the Japanese was moderate while incurring severe damage to their aircraft. While I was there I was able to do some exploring of the nearby military installation, Ft. Mears, and was able to take many pictures of the well- preserved fort. Many of the former soldiers wrote interesting notes on the walls of the buildings. Numerous men were from places like Brooklyn, N.Y. and their forlornness was evident in their graffiti. The barbed wire fences were still in place on the hills overlooking the town as a grim reminder of the War.

Dutch is located near the native Alaskan village of Unalaska and had a population of approximately 4000 in 1970. The commercial fishing revenues from this area are the largest in the western U.S.. Boats from as far away as California ply the waters of the Bering Sea out of Dutch. This King Crab Capital is located approximately 900 miles west of Anchorage in the Aleutian Chain and can only be reached by air or sea.

It was a rare "blue bird" morning when I departed on my first trip to Dutch. The plane was a well worn Grumman Goose amphibian plane - the work horse of the ADF& G fleet. The pilot, Johnny Klingbiel, was a seasoned veteran who formerly flew for several thousand hours with our federal counterpart, The Fish and Wildlife Service. He was noted for making more Dutch runs than anyone else. There is an old Alaskan saying that states that "there are old pilots and there are bold pilots but there ain't no old, bold pilots." Johnny, however, proved to be the exception.

Our flight plan first took us to Kodiak to visit with the warden there then through the Shelikof Straits flying on the south side of the Aleutians. From there we would proceed northward through False Pass (called that because many pilots missed it) to the Bering Sea then through several mountain passes and finally landing at Dutch Harbor. As we proceeded through False Pass the weather changed dramatically. We went from clear skies and unlimited visibility to almost zero visibility. I was privileged to sit in the copilot seat since there was no copilot. It almost felt as though I were flying the plane. That excited as well as frightened me, given the flying conditions.

My fears were somewhat allayed believing that with the help of the flight instruments we would safely reach our destination. I noticed that Johnny was checking his wrist watch very frequently and then glancing at the airspeed indicator. When I asked him why he was doing that he calmly replied: "Well, when you're flying VFR (visual flight rules) you have to do it this way." It's difficult to speak when your chin is on your lap, but I managed to blurt out something to the effect that I thought that we were flying IFR (instrument flight rules). Johnny assured me that was not the case and that I was to be quiet until we reached Dutch. He obviously needed to focus on his somewhat primitive method of navigation.

For the next hour I was frozen to my seat expecting at any moment to slam into an unseen mountainside. Through my dry mouth I uttered a prayer or two and even made some foolish promises to God. There was finally a break in the pea soup fog and I caught my first glimpse of Dutch from an altitude of about 500 feet. The landing was smooth and I started to breathe normally again. My silence with Johnny was broken as I asked him how he managed to get us there without instruments. Later that day, over coffee, he gave the explanation: When flying VFR in the conditions that we were in a few things are absolutely necessary: a good flight map (with topographical features), a compass (usually comes with the plane), a wrist watch, an airspeed indicator and a good dose of courage.

The flight is first charted (laid out) on the map. Then the point at which you lose visual contact is determined on the map. Now the fun begins. The heading is determined by using the map and the compass. By then using the wrist watch and the airspeed indicator the distance along the flight line can be calculated. For example if we were flying due north at 100 miles per hour and we flew for 30 minutes we would have traveled 50 miles. This is perhaps over simplifying the procedure but I hope you get the idea. Johnny had certainly refined this process to the point where he was able to navigate the trip to Dutch Harbor for years without incident.

Johnny no sooner dropped me off then he fueled up and was headed south for False Pass and points east toward Anchorage. "I hope you remembered to wind your watch, Johnny", I thought. I grabbed my army duffel bag and headed for my "reserved spot" at the old deserted bunkhouse near the inactive crab cannery. There was no heat in the building but it was spring and the temperature wouldn't dip much below 40 degrees. My sleeping bag would again serve me well. The next morning found Dutch Harbor immersed in a light fog which dissipated by noon. The early hours had been productive for me; I had located the main crab processor in town, a converted ferry boat from Seattle named "Kalak-ala".

Its body was shiny aluminum, had rows of windows, was about 150 feet long and reminded me of a giant silver minnow. Most of the King Crab boats would bring their catch there rather than going to a distant processor and risking the possible spoilage of their crab. As the boats came in I would board them and inspect for licenses and permits. I would also inspect the crab for size limits and to make sure the crab were not "soft". There is a period of time after the crab, on a yearly cycle, sheds his old shell and grows a new one. Once the new shell starts growing it will be soft and take a few weeks for the shell to harden. The crabs are only partially edible at this time and are illegal to catch or possess.

Later that day I received a tip from one of the locals that a notorious lawbreaker would be docking his crab boat just outside of town. After gaining a description of the boat I headed toward a vantage point near the edge of town. Taking out my binoculars I soon spotted the boat headed my way. Within the hour I was boarding the Kodiak Queen. It was a large boat, about 75 feet long and could carry a cargo of 40,000 lbs. of King Crab, and had a crew of 12. The captain, a burly fellow, unshaven, and in his weathered 40's was surprised to see me, not having been boarded by a warden in a long time. When I asked him if he had much luck, he reported that the crabs were scarce. I offered my sympathies and then asked him to open the ship's hold so I could examine his catch. He sheepishly obliged.

After inspecting several dozen or so of the crabs it was evident that the entire catch of some 40,000 lbs. was soft and therefore illegal! When advised that he was in violation of a fisheries law the captain retorted that he knew they were a little soft but still salvageable. I promptly wrote him a citation and ordered him to put back out to sea where the crab could be dumped back into their natural environment and perhaps have a chance of maturing. He reluctantly agreed and we were soon headed out for the cold and deep waters of the North Pacific. The sea was moderately rough at 6 to 8 feet and I hoped that the journey was short for I was not very sea worthy. As I was stationed at the bow of the ship where I could view the dumping of the crab, a half dozen of the crew gathered around me in an intimidating fashion.

As I faced the crew one of them advised me that it would be very easy to toss me overboard and no one would ever find me. I wasn't sure if he was kidding or not but I shot out a professional reply that my fellow officers knew exactly where I was and with whom. I was bluffing, of course, but they paused a bit then smiled and slowly walked away. They were just testing the young warden's resolve…..or were they? I felt, once again, that Someone was watching over me.

Chapter Four

The Matanuska Moose Massacre

The insurance company lobbyists had won their battle in the state capital, Juneau. Their plea to thin out the Matanuska Valley moose herd, located 30 miles to the east of Anchorage, was soon to become a reality. As the moose herd grew steadily over the last couple of decades, from a few hundred animals to a couple thousand, the incidences of moose versus automobile collisions grew commensurately. And, of course, as the collisions increased, the auto claims paid by the insurance companies increased dramatically as well.

As much as I didn't want to admit it, the grand State of Alaska was about to experience the effect of an eco- political decision that would permanently affect the moose population of the Matanuska Valley. Gone forever would be the day when one could drive along the Glen Highway easterly toward the farming town of Palmer and view several hundred moose leisurely grazing on what was known as the Palmer Hay Flats. They would have been driven down out of their summer haunts in the Chugach Mountains by the heavy snows commencing in late October making them vulnerable to their sheet metal assailants.

I could somewhat justify thinning out the herd to protect the public but the order that the Department received from the governor's office was that some 1000+ animals would need to be harvested in a permit- only hunt. The plan was not to just thin the herd out, it was to decimate it, that is to reduce it to a point that with continued hunting seasons the herd would never recover to its former numbers but would be sustained at more "manageable" numbers, perhaps a few hundred. A similar tactic, against the opinions of ADF&G wildlife biologists, was conducted a few years prior on the Kenai Peninsula, well- known as "a million acre moose ranch" where the hunt was later described as a "bloodbath". The herd there has never recovered sufficiently to afford much in the way of trophy hunting.

The hunt occurred, to the best of my memory, on an early February weekend in 1970. After spending a restless night in a drafty colonial hotel in Palmer I assumed my post on the Hay Flats well before daylight on Saturday morning. It was a cold gray morning and the sun seemed to struggle to lift its head above the towering mountains to the east; maybe it didn't want to witness the slaughter either. The hunter's vehicles were lined up for miles and the permit holders were taking their last sips of hot coffee before loading their weapons.

The moose had spent the night lying asleep on the frozen tundra totally unaware of what awaited them. Humanely, the hunt regulations stated that moose calves and cows with calves could not be harvested; only calf less cows and bulls. As the first rays of daylight peeked over the ridges the first "pop" was heard quickly followed by the sounds of gun shots reverberating throughout the Valley. The volley was nearly non- stop for the first hours then slowing to an occasional "crack" and then an eery silence. The slaughter was over as quickly as it had begun; the permits had been filled. The rest of the day was spent counting carcasses and gut piles to estimate as accurately as possible the total kill. By nightfall me and my fellow wardens and biologists estimated that approximately 1100 moose had been killed in that one day. Only a few calves had been shot and as I remember the oldest cow moose, judging by her teeth, was 16 years old, well past her prime breeding years. Over 40 years has passed since that infamous day and sadly it still remains fresh in my mind. In 2007 my family and I visited the beautiful Matanuska Valley and saw only a few moose- the remnant of what used to be and will be no more.

Chapter Five

Russian River Reds

The Russian River located on the Kenai Peninsula about 150 miles south of Anchorage, is home to one of the largest Sockeye Salmon fisheries in the world. The sockeye, also known as the red salmon is arguably the best eating, especially when smoked, of the 5 species found in Alaska. The other 4 species, in descending order of edibility, are the Silver or Coho, the King or Chinook, the Dog or Chum, and lastly the Pink or Humpy Salmon. The largest in the Cook Inlet Fishery is the King, averaging about 25 lbs., the Chum next at 10 lbs., the Silver at 7 lbs. the Red at 6 lbs. and the Pink at about 3.5 lbs.

The Russian River was at one time, prior to 1970, noted as a top- shelf Rainbow Trout fishery, regularly reporting trophies weighing 10lbs. or more. Fishing pressure over the years has caused it to be now considered a non – trophy Rainbow fishery, rarely producing anything over 5 lbs. The Russian is only about 5 miles in length, from its beginning at the mouth of Russian Lake to its confluence with the famed Kenai River, home of the largest King Salmon on the planet as well as trophy Rainbow Trout.

When I went to work for the ADF&G in 1969 there was no sport fishery on the Russian River although the fish were certainly there. The complaint was that the Reds were not sport fish and could not be caught by conventional sporting methods as opposed to the subsistence method of snagging. There were, however, some fishery biologists employed by the State who contended that they had caught Reds on weighted streamers called Coho flies. In June of 1969 a few of us decided to try the flies out and with a little instruction we were soon catching our limit and having a great time contending the hard-fighting fish.

The Russian River fishery, as well as the nearby streams had at one time earned the reputation for being a "combat-fishing zone". One would have to actually see this fishery to fully appreciate the drama. Picture, if you would, anglers standing shoulder- to shoulder for 100 yards or so, on both sides of the stream casting "Russian River flies" at the fish. These specially made "flies" were not fishing flies at all but merely large treble hooks with lead weights affixed to them.

The idea was to cast the hook into the midst of the school of fish and then jerk it through the mass and then "horse" the fish onto the bank of the stream. Bear in mind that during the height of the fish run the fish are so thick that it would be virtually impossible to cast a hook and not snag a salmon! Where the idea of "combat" came into play was when the fish would be superficially impaled by the treble hook and then during the ensuing struggle the hook would come loose and then be propelled by the force of the bent fishing rod backwards toward the innocent bystanders! The velocity of the hooked-projectile was incredible and combined with several ounces of lead it became a potentially deadly missile! Although I never saw or heard of anyone being killed by the "fly" I can certainly attest to a few people being maimed. Most projectiles were warded off by thick clothing and hats; others by ducking and dodging which became a sport in itself. During an afternoon of "fishing" it was not unusual to see a couple of fishermen impaled by the leaded hook. Some were removed on the spot with a trusty pair of pliers while others required a trip to the ER several miles away in the towns of Kenai or Soldotna.

I can vividly recall a warm (60+ degree) sunny day in June of 1969 or 70 during the first run of Reds on the Russian River. In a sense I was still a rookie warden but no means a novice at fishing. For that reason I was chosen to patrol the busiest part of the river which at the mouth where it flowed into the mighty Kenai. The fish were thick and I was fortunate that a law prohibiting the use of weighted treble hooks was in now effect. I had had my share of close calls with the projectiles and wanted no more. I soon settled into enjoying the sight of fisherman catching beautiful red salmon in a sporting fashion. The fish were scrappy belying their modest weight of 6 or 7 lbs.

About midday I a heard a commotion upstream accented by the sound of fishermen scrambling out of the stream. Not to my surprise I noticed a mature cow moose, 5-6 feet at the shoulder, sauntering down the stream occasionally dipping her massive head beneath the water to nip off an unknown delicacy. She seemed to be completely oblivious of the crowd, apparently knowing that it wasn't moose hunting season.

I then proceeded to yell to the crowd that a moose was coming down the stream and that she had the right of way. I further cautioned everyone to pull in their lines so as not to hook the moose. As one should expect there always has to be someone that feels that a warden is a necessary evil and that he is not to be taken seriously.

Well, as you might guess he hooked the cow in the flank and quickly informed everyone: "moose on!" The moose undoubtedly felt the sting of the hook and took off down the stream scattering fishermen as she ran with the careless fisherman in hot pursuit. The sight of the man tripping and falling into the stream several times, the sound of the drag on his reel zinging, and the roar of laughter is indelibly inscribed in my mind. I soon put an end to the contest by cutting the line, much to the dismay of the fisherman! After listening to him complaining about losing his favorite fly my patience wore thin and I informed him that I was about ready to cite him for attempting to bag a moose out of season and for using illegal means. He quietly returned to his former station on the river bank feeling rather foolish I would assume.

Sadly, that was the last time that I patrolled the Russian as I was transferred to another district the following year. The fishery at the Russian River still thrives to this day thanks to the wise management of the resource by the ADF&G.

Chapter Six

The Seal That Barked

A quiet spring afternoon was interrupted by an urgent phone call from a diner/gas station near Girdwood, a well –known ski resort located 50 miles south of Anchorage on the Turnagain Arm. Before you ask I will inform you where the term "turnagain" originated. Legend has it (Alaska is the Land of Legends) that Captain Cook in his search for a Northwest Passage navigated his ship into this large bay which is a finger of the Cook Inlet which was ,of course, named for him. After sailing up the arm for several miles, the ship nearly ran aground in the shallow tidewater and he gave the order to "turnagain" or in our lingo, turnaround. It is easy to understand Cook's near disaster when one learns that the tides in the Cook Inlet area can reach 30 feet or more at certain times of the year. It is a common mistake to sail in at high tide, anchor and forget that when the tide ebbs you will end up high and dry.

The woman on the phone was frantically trying to explain to me that a man was beating a seal with a club on the tide flats near the diner. I assured her that I would be there within the hour and if she could try to detain the man. Seals were protected by the Marine Mammals Act of 1972 but this being 1969 the seals had a hunting season on them, however, the season was closed and the area we were in was closed to seal hunting period. Being the zealous warden that I was I made haste south on the narrow and curvy Seward Highway at what I deemed a reasonable and prudent speed; an Alaska State Trooper thought otherwise and pulled behind me with red lights flashing.

I very reluctantly pulled over and as I rolled down my window I offered a few expletives regarding his lack of courtesy in pulling a fellow officer over. He, being a fellow rookie, proceeded to tell me of his duties to protect the public. Feeling very impressed to get on with my duties I informed him that I was moving on and if he interrupted me again he had better call for reinforcements. Twenty minutes later I arrived at the scene of the alleged violation with no Troopers in sight. By this time the lady who had called me had the perpetrator seated at the diner enjoying some coffee and home-made pie. After introducing myself I cautioned him to stay put while I walked out to the mud flats to see if I could find the seal.

About a hundred yards out I found the seal, a Spotted Seal, bleeding from the nose and having a serious contusion on the side of its head. I had no choice but to dispatch the poor animal with a single shot from my.38. I then dragged the 100 lb. carcass to my vehicle to be held for evidence. Now the story gets interesting. When I interviewed the man and asked him what caused him to club the seal he said that it scared him when he attempted to photograph it.

I informed him that the defenseless creature was probably scared too and that he would be cited for the unlawful act. I then handed him the citation and told him that I would see him in court in a few days.

The judge in court that day was notoriously hard on tourists that did stupid things. When the man was asked to approach the bench and explain his side of the story he explained to the judge that as he walked toward the seal to photograph it, the seal "barked" at him and frightened him so much that he picked up a piece of drift wood and beat him with it. I can't recall all that the judge said but I do know that it wasn't pretty and it cost the tourist 500 dollars. I felt sorry for the guy and just couldn't bring myself to ask him how the picture of the seal turned out.

Chapter Seven

Clam Diggin' Cheechakos

For those of you who aren't familiar with the term "cheechako" it is a uniquely Alaskan expression meaning "green horn" or more literally, a person who is not familiar with the challenges of life on the Last Frontier. The antithesis of a "cheechako" would be a "sourdough", or one who has spent some time in Alaska and survived. Alaskan tradition says that in order to become a real sourdough a man must first, kiss a grizzly bear, second, swim across the Yukon River and third, marry an Indian princess. Only a few have attained that status, and one notably, met with disaster when he confused steps one and three! OK, on with the clam diggers!

I was returning from a fishing patrol on the Kenai Peninsula one early summer afternoon in 1970 and driving north on the Seward Highway along Turnagain Arm when I noticed what appeared to be 3 figures on the tidal flats several hundred yards from shore. That was highly unusual for there was no good reason for them to be there. I then put my binoculars on them and was able to clearly make out three men who were apparently making an attempt at digging clams. Obviously unknown to them was the fact that there were no clams indigenous to that area- but what would you expect from Cheechakos?

Remembering that the tidal flats in the Cook Inlet area are notorious for taking the lives of careless and unsuspecting adventurers, I quickly checked my tide book. High tide was due in 2 hours which meant that the tide would start rolling in at any time. There were numerous channels between the men and the shore that would fill with tide water before they could reach shore leaving them victims of the frigid muddy waters. I had to act fast. I got on the 2-way radio in my vehicle and told dispatch to call the military rescue team at nearby Elmendorf AFB and request an emergency status rescue. After giving them my precise location I then tried to get the attention of the endangered trio. No yelling could get their attention and trying to reach them by foot would be foolish because of the muddy ooze of the tidal flat that would act as quicksand if you stepped in the wrong spot.

After repeated honks on the department wagon they looked my way and I did my best to wave them on toward shore. Surprisingly, they heeded my gestures and slowly headed toward shore. In the distance I could hear the chop- chop of the Air Force helicopter heading our way. It was going to be very close. As soon as the men were within the sound of my voice, I encouraged them to run as fast as they could for the tide was rolling in fast. When they looked behind them a saw the tide closing in they dropped all their gear and made haste.

When 50 yards from shore they were cut off by a flooded tidal channel which was impassible. They now had no choice but to swim to safety. They reluctantly inched into the numbing cold water and splashed the 20 yards across the channel - undoubtedly what would be the longest swim of their lives. Finally they staggered, stiffened by the cold water, across the final few yards to the waiting chopper. The cheechakos seemed visibly shaken by the ordeal but not physically harmed. To be safe they were flown to the Elmendorf Hospital where they were treated for exposure and released to clam again; hopefully not on the mudflats at Turnagain.

Chapter Eight

Bad Luck in the Alaska Range

E arly August marks the beginning of sheep season in most parts of Alaska. It is the "hunt above hunts" and is reserved for the most determined and hardiest of hunters. The targeted sheep are "ovis dalli" or the highly- prized Dall Sheep and are found in all of the State's major mountain ranges. The record sheep was shot in 1961 by the late Harry Swank in the Wrangell Mountains and measured a whopping 189 plus points by the official Boone and Crockett standard. Only an average of seven sheep a year score 160 points or more.

I was excited to be chosen to conduct a sheep patrol near the headwaters of the Healy River in the Alaska Range. The plan was to fly me in by chopper and set up a base camp on one of the ridges from which I could establish visual contact with the hunters on the surrounding mountains by use of binoculars and a 60 power spotting scope. At daybreak on opening day the chopper, piloted by a Viet Nam veteran, dropped me and my gear off atop a barren peak overlooking the Healy River Valley. My gear was sparse: sleeping bag, 30-06 rifle (for bear protection), warm clothes, spotting gear, jerky and dried fruit, climbing boots and a Buck folding knife- enough to sustain me for the 3 days that I was expected to stay there.

During the stay I was to watch for hunters who might shoot a sheep the same day in which they were airborne which was illegal, to check for appropriate licenses and tags and to enforce the law that required any bagged sheep to have at least a ½ horn curl.

I hadn't quite finished setting up camp when I heard the distinct sound of light plane flying up the river valley. The plane flew over me in the direction of large band of sheep two miles distant that I had spotted earlier. I watched the Piper Super Cub land deftly about a mile from me between me and the sheep.

The pilot/ hunter obviously thought that I was just another hunter as I revealed no identifying ADF&G marks- in other words I was working "undercover". I decided to observe the hunter to see if he bothered to set up camp which would be the basic MO for most legal hunters. I trained my 12x Bushnells on the hunter and noticed that he was alone and made no attempt to set up camp but quickly set off in the direction of the sheep. I then set up my 60x spotting scope and watched him stalk the sheep very carefully being careful to only walk in their direction when the heads of the older rams were down. The eyesight of the sheep is incredibly keen, equal to that of a 10x binocular.

Anything within a mile is perceived as a danger to them; so it is paramount that the hunter keeps a very low profile even if it necessitates crawling on his belly. After an hour or so of stalking, the hunter was able to hide himself behind a small boulder and soon I heard the crack of the high- powered rifle.

I noticed one of the rams about 200 yards from him jerk, take a few short steps then fold to the mossy ground. It didn't appear to be a trophy ram, but nonetheless, illegal. I quickly trained the spotting scope on the plane and was able to clearly make out its license numbers which would be used as evidence. I then watched the hunter approach the ram, take a few pictures and proceed to eviscerate then skin it. It was time for me to quickly make my way to the plane to intercept the violator before he could make off with the illegal sheep. I made good time on the open, rocky terrain and was calmly sitting on one of the Super Cub's over-sized tundra tires when the tired hunter arrived with a shocked look on his face. "Hello, I'm officer Huba from the ADF&G" was my greeting.

His reply was, "Oh, s--t!" He continued, "How the ---- did you know that I was here?" I replied, "Well, you did fly over my camp didn't you?" He was nonplussed and slowly dropped his would- be prize to the ground. I then wrote out a citation for shooting a sheep the same day while airborne and placed a seizure tag on the sheep carcass. The plan was then for him to fly back to his home base, Anchorage, and then appear in court a few days later. I bid the sad hunter adieu, then proceeded to pack the sheep to my camp.

After the hunter regained his composure I could hear the Cub's engine sputter then roar as the plane started down the short, rocky make- shift runway. I've always liked to watch small aircraft take off and this was no exception. As I watched, I quickly noticed that the plane was having trouble getting airborne. After traveling some 300 feet and gaining only about 6 feet in altitude the pilot decided to return the craft back to terra firma.

Not noticing a fair- sized rock in his path he hit it squarely nosing the plane into the earth and flipping it over onto its back. Hoping that the fuel tanks were not ruptured, I ran toward the crippled bird as fast as the rocky terrain would allow.

A minute later I was peering through the Plexiglas door window at the pilot hanging upside down from his safety harness and hearing him speak loudly in some profane tongue. When he finally noticed me watching him his look was a mixture of "not you again" and "glad to see someone." Fortunately, the door was not damaged and opened easily as I reached in to help extricate the unfortunate hunter. It was apparent that the only damage he suffered was to his pride, which I could understand all too well. Without talking we gathered his gear from the plane and made the short trek to my campsite. Over a cup of hastily brewed mountain coffee we recounted the happenings of the day.

As it turned out he was a decent chap and admitted his recent bad choices, one, killing the sheep illegally and two, allowing his anger to cloud his judgment on takeoff causing him to not properly "choke" the plane's carburetor.

The following morning the chopper arrived and flew us back to headquarters in Fairbanks. The hunter made his scheduled court appearance 2 days later and was unfortunate enough to stand before a surly judge. Overriding my recommendations as well as the D.A.'S the hunter was slapped with a 500.00 fines and loss of hunting license for that year and the next. Coupled with a wrecked plane atop a mountain, the penalty would be one that he would remember for a long time.

Part Three

The Days Before the ADF&G

Chapter One

A Boone & Crockett Sheep

Perhaps there was no other animal taken from the annals of *Field and Stream* and *Outdoor Life* that stirred my blood as much as sheep: Mongolian, Stone, Desert and of course, Dall. My dream of hunting them, all of them, punctuated much of my early days in Pennsylvania vaguely remembering that much of real life is built upon boyhood dreams. But how could I actually live my dream? I was a college grad working in a dirty steel mill in a dead end job alongside hundreds of other dead- ended men who also at one time also had dreams. What made me any different from them?

I knew that if I were to live out my dream it would have to begin soon or I would end up like all the others. What made me different? I can only think of one thing- the will of God. God had planted that desire, that dream within me and I could not shake it, I could only make it happen. I prophetically proclaimed to my mill buddies what I was going to do in the Last Frontier and their reaction was one not unlike that of Biblical Joseph's brothers! I promised to send them pictures which might compel them to follow me. I sent but the best never came; they had mill sludge in their veins, I had mountain spring water in mine -the kind that mountain sheep drink. So long and good luck to you ol' mill buddies.

In the spring of 1966 with over 5000 miles between my old life and my new I met up with my old Army buddy, Ron Sturgeon and soon we were planning our first Dall sheep hunt together. Ron was nearly as addicted to hunting as I was; perhaps he acquired his addiction in the farmland of Pennsylvania as I had. We spent most of the spring and early summer devising the perfect powder and bullet combinations that would fell our Dalls. As I recall, I settled for a 150 grain Sierra Boat Tail bullet fueled by a now forgotten powder charge. The rifle was a 30-06 cal. Husqvarna Sporter Lightweight rifle, touted as the ideal mountain rifle. What I needed was a flat shooting rifle with good accuracy out to 500 yards. After weeks of range shooting I was able to get consistent ¾ inch groups at 150 yards. At 300 yards the groups widened to 2 inches which I felt was sufficient. I didn't practice at further ranges but trusted that I could extrapolate if necessary.

Both Ron and I desired to bag a record book sheep. The "book" is the famous Boone & Crockett Record Book for North American Big Game Animals. In order to make the book the sheep would have to score 160 points or better. A half dozen or so make the book each year attesting to the fact of how difficult it really is. With that in mind we would some homework to do. We decided to start by talking with the local taxidermists, who if anyone, would be privy to the best hunting spots.

We soon learned that serious sheep hunters form a closed circle of comrades who are rather protective of their ranks and their records. Therefore, most of the information we gleaned was very general in nature only divulging mountain ranges in which the sheep were shot or on occasion the river drainage was mentioned. We would somehow have to break into the "elite information bank." As good fortune would have it, I discovered that my land lord, Gene Effler, was an avid sheep hunter and in fact held the #7 position in the book, and to boot, his friends held most of the top 10 positions!

He was surely the man to talk to. In addition to being my landlord, Gene was also my boss since I was the manager for his apartment complexes. I guess that set the stage for a particular relationship. After a couple of racks of Kodiak Island deer ribs washed down with some Pacific Northwest beer Gene seemed more willing to share his secrets; however, I had to promise not to tell anyone else. I did promise and I hoped that he didn't see me cross my fingers, eyes and legs thus invalidating the promise! Gene proceeded to show me pictures of the top 10 sheep. He showed me Harry Swank's #1, then #3, then his, #7 etc. and then asked what I saw in the pictures.

I replied, "really big sheep." "Look closely at their horns, Al, what do you see?" I then noticed that the horns were all similar in curl shape, breadth and length. Gene then informed me that they all came from the same the same geographic area, in fact, from the same 25 square miles area! I thanked him then reminded him that Alaska was large, in fact, 586,000 square miles large. He nodded, reminding me again not to tell anyone, then produced a topographical map of the McCarthy area of south central Alaska and started to pin point the big sheep area. In the early summer of 1968 Ron and I started serious preparations for our hunt. We planned to drive to a place from which we could fly within hiking then climbing distance from the sheep. The town we picked was Chitina located about 20 miles west of our drop off point.

Chitina is located on the west bank of the Copper River at its confluence with the Chitina River on the Edgerton Highway, and junction with the McCarthy Road. It is 53 miles southeast of Copper Center and 66 miles southeast of Glennallen just outside the western boundary of the Wrangell - St Elias National Park and Preserve. Chitina is located on the west bank of the Copper River at its confluence with the Chitina River on the Edgerton Highway and the junction with the McCarthy Road. It is 53 mi southeast of Copper Center and 66 miles southeast of Glennallen.

Athabascans have lived in the area around Chitina for centuries as evidenced by the archaeological sites south and east of Chitina. Before 1900, Chitina was the site of large village whose population was slowly decimated by the influx of people, disease and conflicts. Copper ore was discovered in about 1900 along the northern edge of the Chitina River valley. This brought a rush of prospectors and homesteaders to the area. The Copper River and Northwestern Railway enabled Chitina to develop into a thriving community by 1914.

It had a general store, a clothing store, a meat market, stables, a tinsmith, five hotels, several rooming houses, a pool hall, bars, restaurants, dance halls and a movie theater. The mines closed in 1938 and the remaining support activities moved to what is now the Glennallen area. Chitina became a virtual ghost town. Otto Adrian Nelson, a surveying engineer for the Kennecott Mines, eventually bought up much of the town. He built a unique hydroelectric system that supplied electric power to all his buildings.

He also supplied much of the town center with hot and cold running water. Current activity in Chitina revolves around the dipnet fishing for salmon that occurs every summer. Alaskans are allowed to dip a large number of salmon during their spawning runs and Chitina is an accessible and popular place for this activity. Now that I've described the town to you it would be best to advise you that if you do visit Chitina, do not plan on sheep hunting from that point, for several million acres of prime sheep territory has been placed within the sanctuary of the Wrangell-St.Elias Mountain Wildlife Preserve. It is certain that at this time there wanders in the refuge at least one ram that would outrank Harry Swank's world record. Rest in peace, Mr. Swank, knowing that your record is safe…. for now.

The next part of our plan was to find a pilot who would fly us to our destination which would be difficult for most of the pilots in that area would be flying other sheep hunters who had booked their hunts a year or two in advance. After checking with other flight services in the Chitina area we located a young pilot by the name of Kenny Lithgoe. (Why I would remember his name after 45 years is a mystery to me) He advised us that he did not own a plane but could probably lease one at a reasonable price. The plane turned out to be a Cessna 185 on floats. We chose a plane on floats (pontoons) knowing that that was what we would need to land on a small lake approximately 6 miles from our proposed hunting area. From there we would follow some old mining trails into the Wrangells.

Choosing gear and packing was never a chore for me- it was always exciting discovering and packing the necessities for the hunt and some things that were not so essential such as a few Hersey bars. Packing the right tent for sheep hunting was important; it had to be lightweight and waterproof. Mine was purchased at Barney Seiler's Mountain Sporting Goods in Anchorage; it was expensive, made of Egyptian cotton, whose fibers swell when wet and had a waterproof floor. It was perfect for one occupant but in a pinch two could fit. A good folding knife was essential; mine was a Buck with a 4 inch blade.

It was difficult to sharpen but held an edge and later proved valuable in sub zero weather in that it wouldn't break. A Thermalite sleeping pad was necessary especially when a hunter had to establish a "spike camp" which was a temporary overnight camp which was used when one could not make it back to camp. Food was primarily freeze-dried meals, extremely lightweight and just needing water for preparation. An axe, spotting scope, binoculars, 50 feet of nylon rope, matches in a waterproof case, toilet articles, a Primus mountain stove, a quart of kerosene, small flashlight (seldom used due to 18hours of daylight in August), metal eating utensils, mountain boots, and 2 changes of warm clothes rounds out the short list. Warm woolen clothes were a must when hunting @ 6- 7000 feet for it can drop below freezing at night.

Accompanying Ron and I was his younger brother, Tim, a young, tough farm boy from our home state of Pennsylvania. The drive from Anchorage to Chitina took about 6 hours and was extraordinarily picturesque since it was a "blue bird" day. We located our pilot, Kenny, and arranged for a short recon trip over our sheep area 15 miles to the east. Following our topo map we quickly located the area where the "big boys" were reputed to live. Within minutes we were able to locate several bands of ewes and lambs which did not travel with the rams at this time of year.

Coursing over a few ridges we finally spotted a band of 12 rams. Flying just low enough to gage the horn sizes but not spook the sheep unduly, we noted that 6 of the rams were legal, having at least half curls, one of which stood out above the rest. We informed Kenny that we were after a record book sheep and he informed us that the lead ram was of that caliber. Just make sure we had him make another pass at the rams. The 2nd pass confirmed that guess; he was at least a full curl, well over 40 inches with heavy bases. My heart was pounding heavily and I knew we were to expect a sleepless night. A Boone and Crockett ram was just a few hours away! We excitedly returned to Chitina and grabbed a room at the storied Chitina Hotel. The supper was what one could expect in such surroundings- miner/ prospector style!

I was awake well before daylight the next morning and made my way down the creaky stairs to where the coffee was brewing. My partners soon followed and we hurriedly wolfed down the bacon, eggs and hash browns- the last full meal we would enjoy for the next week. Kenny soon showed up in his battered 4 wheel drive truck and we were on our way to the point of departure- a small lake at town's edge. Having carefully packed a few days later we tossed our 75# backpacks into the back of the truck and proceeded down a bumpy mining road to the lake.

The day was cool (50 degrees) and overcast which was ideal for both flying and hiking. At the lake we got a look at the bird that was going to fly us to another small lake a few miles away from which we would start our ascent into the mountains. The Cessna 185 was well-equipped to launch 3 hunters and their gear plus the pilot into the air over a surprisingly short distance. Kenny pointed the nose of the plane due east into the misty sun and we slowly rose to our desired altitude of about 1500 feet- no need to fly higher for the short 10 minute flight. The landscape was dotted with lakes of all sizes and I was impressed at how Kenny was able to pick out the right one. We soon splashed down gently and taxied toward the eastern birch- lined shore. I deplaned first and then the guys traversed the pontoon and handed me the 75 # backpacks which seemed light then but would feel much heavier as we made our climb to Elliot Creek some 10 miles distant. We waved to Kenny as he dipped the wings of the 185 as a way of saying "see you in a week."

We took out our topographical maps and compasses and knelt on the sandy beach to get our bearings. The training that Ron and I both had with the Alaska National Guard Recon Unit would serve us well. The maps we had were dated but accurate, however, they did not tell us that the old mining trails were long overgrown with alder bushes. The brush was in fact thicker on the trails than off the trails so we quickly decided to walk along the trails rather than on them. In most places we could see no further than 10 feet, making it necessary to check our compasses frequently to assure that we were headed in the right direction.

We had no view of the mountains so we went strictly by the compass. Early in the afternoon, as it warmed up, the mosquitoes showed up, not in singles nor pairs, but in legions! We were somewhat prepared (there is no such thing as being fully prepared). Preferring the liquid repellant over the spray we applied generous portions to all exposed areas of our bodies, especially around the ears and neck. The first day in the brush was very taxing; between our heavy packs constantly getting hung up in the brush and the skeeters getting into our noses and eyes, the progress was slow.

There were numerous grizzly and wolf tracks in the muddy trail we were on. We fully expected to come face to face with a bear; the wolves most generally shy away from humans. By late that evening of our first day we reached the base of the mountains, tired, sweaty, and itchy from the 100s of mosquito bites we suffered. We washed nearby in an ice cold brook that tumbled down over the boulders near the mountain.

Refreshed, we were ready to try our first freeze dried meal. I don't remember what it was but I'm sure that there was some kind of name for it. We reveled in the thought of sheep back straps roasting over an open birch fire. That, however, would have to wait. The only open space available for our sleeping bags was a game trail that led to the brook; a poor choice but being exhausted we crawled into our bags and covered our faces as best we could to guard us against the incessant insects.

At daybreak the next morning, after downing some hot tea and crackers, we excitedly shouldered our packs grabbed our rifles and headed into the cold dew- covered brush. As we hiked upward the brush slowly thinned out and we were soon greeted with a fast panorama of rocks and boulders interspersed with lush verdant grass and several varieties of wild flowers. As we progressed, it was no longer a hike but a climb. Although it was in the high 40s, beads of sweat soon appeared on our faces but fortunately we had left the mosquitoes behind us. Soon our legs muscles were burning and as we ascended into the higher altitude our breathing became more labored. We were glad that not only were we young but our daily regimen of running had paid off. After several hours of climbing we finally reached a mountain peak with a cliff overlooking The Creek from which we could look for the sheep. We unloaded our gear set up a rough camp then got down to the business of spotting our prey. Within just a few minutes we were able to spot the band of rams that we had seen from the air. They were about ½ mile away in a valley below us feeding casually near The Creek.

We decided to stalk the sheep from a position downstream from them since the terrain between us was too steep to traverse. In order to reach the creek we would have to walk along a knife ridge for ½ mile being careful to stay on the narrow sheep trail that extended along the top. I cautioned my 2 partners to slow the pace so as not to lose our footing. The words were just out of my mouth when I heard Ron stumble behind me. I turned quickly to see Ron start to roll down the steep slide. Fortunately he was carrying a lighter pack and was able splay his legs and slow his roll, finally digging in his boot heels and coming to a heart thumping stop.

Tim and I offered to come to his aid but Ron assured us that he was ok. Back on the trail an examination revealed only a few scrapes to his knees and elbows and a noticeable ding to his pride. We continued with our stalk and within an hour we were at the base of the mountain near the Creek a quarter mile from our prey. Somewhere in my studies of sheep hunting an expert advised that the hunter should wear a white set of "baker's clothes" so as to fool the sheep into thinking that you are "cousins coming to visit." So much for the expert advice; we hadn't moved but a few yards when the lead ram spotted us and hightailed it to higher ground with 11 of his subjects in pursuit.

Since they were now out of rifle range, we had no choice now but to back track and assume our positions near the peak where we were a few hours ago. Thankfully, it was still early in the day so there was no rush. As we started our climb up the knife ridge I suddenly felt the sole of my left boot separate. Obviously this was a serious development since operable boots are a necessity for mountain hunting. After some thought I decided to use 1/8 inch nylon cord in an effort to secure the sole to the boot. Amazingly, it worked and we were on our way! The cord only had to be changed a couple of time afterwards.

Recently observing the incredibly keen eyesight of the animals we decided to try to keep entirely out of sight as nearly as was possible. This would necessitate us placing the knife ridge between us and them. Since it would be impossible to walk on the steep side of the knife ridge we would have to find another way. A check of the topo map revealed that there was a small valley on the other side of the ridge that would lead us to within ½ mile of our destination. It was surely be the long way around, but it would soon prove to be the right choice. It was early afternoon now and the temperature was in the 70s, too warm for climbing. Within a couple of hours we were sweat soaked and in need of refreshment.

The small brook in the valley didn't offer much help but we spotted something that would- a large snow bank on the far side of the valley that seemed to have a cave at its front! It was several hundred yards away and we were there in just minutes. We weren't disappointed for the cave was large, 20 feet wide at the entrance and extending some 50 or 60 feet to the rear. The cave was the result of melting snow higher up forming a small stream that undercut its way through the snow eventually forming the cave. The snow bank itself seemed to be the result of an avalanche of a few years ago.

The temperature in the cave seemed to be in the 50's and we cooled quickly and were soon ready to continue our journey. After being refreshed we quickened our pace and arrived at the peak by late afternoon. We were able to spot the sheep across the valley ½ mile away. We decided that since it was late in the day the best thing to do would be to hunker down and wait and see if the sheep would move closer. Our hunch was right- the band was moving toward the creek to get their evening drink.

They stopped about 800 yards away. We agreed that this was as close to them as we had been all day but they were still out of rifle range. Should we attempt to get closer or call it a day? We then saw a rocky outcropping below us that, if reached, would gain us another 100 yards or so. Knowing that sheep are alert to predators coming from below them we felt confident that they would not see us coming at them from several hundred above them at a 45 degree angle. It was a treacherous decent and we were careful not to dislodge any boulders that may alert them. Arriving there we estimated that we were still approximately 700 yards from them at an angle of 45 degrees. Both Ron and Tim agreed that it was too far and the angle was bad. I disagreed and was confident that although it was a difficult shot it was well within the realm of possibility. They both finally agreed that if I had the confidence then I should go for it.

I took off my pack and used it for my rifle rest. I then had to calculate my shot: 700 yards @ a 45 degree angle. I hadn't planned for this kind of a shot! I had practiced at 300 yards and after studying the ballistics of my rifle and bullet match I was certain that with a little good fortune I could hit a sheep @ 500 yards – on a flat plane. This was 700 yards @ a 45 degree angle! After some deliberate head calculations I got into a prone shooting position aided by the outcropping and my pack. I placed the scope's crosshairs just above the ram's front shoulder, took a deep breath, exhaled slowly until my breath stopped and gently squeezed the trigger.

We saw the dust fly and we all agreed that the shot was low- but how low? As I was recalculating, the sheep limped forward a few steps and stopped. Placing the spotting scope on him we noticed that his left front leg was broken at the knee. I made the adjustment and fired again; as the rifle's report echoed throughout the valley the monarch took a few steps and crumpled onto the grassy carpet. At the fall of their leader the other sheep panicked; half of them headed our way! Ron and Tim took up their positions and within a few minutes both guys bagged full curl rams! At this point, as the sun was setting, we decided to wait until the following morning to retrieve our prizes. It would prove to be a worrisome night- would the grizzlies or wolves find our sheep while we slept?

We were up at the crack of dawn after sharing a restless night. There was no time for breakfast; the vanquished were waiting for the victors! Arriving at the kill site we were relieved to find our trophies intact. I quickly pulled out my measuring tape, that I just so happened to have along, and took the necessary measurement to see if it qualified for the record book. I determined an unofficial score of 173 and ½, well above the minimum entry score of 160. After the horns dried out for 60 days the horns would then be officially scored. In this case the official score would be 172 and 7/8, good enough for 105th place all time in the Book. It was with a mixture of both elation and sadness that we packed our animals back to camp.

For the next few days we gorged ourselves on sheep meat: back straps, steaks, the heart, kidneys, brains, yes, even the Rocky Mountain Oysters (testicles). In my opinion mountain sheep meat is the finest of wild game cuisine. A couple of days later we met our pilot at the small lake which we found easily once again using our compasses. Our packs were noticeably heavier coming out due to the addition of the sheep meat so by the time we reached the lake we were once again soaked with sweat.

The cold water of the lake was a welcome bath for us as we shed a week's worth of grime. Back at Chitina as we were unloading our meat and gear from the plane we were greeted by an old Swede who in the 1930s was a cook for a nearby and now deserted mining camp. When asked what he thought about my trophy sheep he smiled as he dryly replied: "Nice for camp meat; used to shoot them kind all the time." My grandfather never did like Swedes.

Chapter Two

Kenai Peninsula Mountain Goats

Steve Pavish was an avid goat hunter who had spent some time hunting for trophies in Southeastern Alaska. Although I had just come off a very successful sheep hunt, Steve enticed me into going on a follow up hunt to the rugged coastal mountains on the Kenai Peninsula about 150 miles south of Anchorage. We would be hunting out of Port Dick some 25 miles south of the quaint town of Homer. The area was seldom hunted since access was very difficult, therefore, was a good bet for trophy goats.

Steve was sure that I could bag a trophy goat perhaps even a record book goat with horns exceeding 10 inches. To increase my chances he even volunteered to not hunt himself but to act as my guide.

Our launching point would be from the harbor in Homer flying with the fabled Homer Air service. The pilot was a young buck with only a few hundred hours under his belt which made me nervous for the weather looked foreboding that morning. After a bumpy take off from salt water, things really got interesting as we bounced and bucked our way south. I'm glad the flight only lasted 30 minutes or so for my breakfast was near my throat when we finally landed at Port Dick. It was raining now accented by a 20 mph wind- not exactly a nice day for hunting.

We donned our waterproof nylon rain gear and headed for a stand of tall Sitka Spruce 50 yards from shore. Somewhat sheltered from the rain we made some last minute plans for the hunt. Our hunt would take us from sea level to about 3500 feet over what seemed to be vertical terrain! At the first sign of a break in the weather we headed for a steep slope near us. The going was rough, much more so than on the sheep hunt since there was no trail to follow- we had to break trail the whole way.

The rain had made the climbing treacherous; moss covered rocks had to be gingerly coursed and grassy patches were like sliding boards. The climb was greatly aided by grabbing limbs above us then pulling ourselves up. Early in the climb I noticed a plethora of broomstick- like plants of some kind growing between the trees. They were particularly inviting since they were about 1 ½ inches in diameter- perfect for a hand hold.

I eagerly grabbed hold of one above me and pulled up; the pain was almost instant. My un-gloved hand was soon turning red and filled with tiny spines. I had innocently grabbed hold of the climber's nemesis- Echinopanax horridus, otherwise known as Devil's Club. Used as a medicine by Alaskans it was now an "anti- medicine." For the next 20 minutes I plucked out as many spines as I could, applied some first-aid ointment and warily continued climbing. The greenhorn had learned another lesson in Alaskan wood lore. The sound of "Cheechako!!" seemed to ring off the mountain.

Four soggy hours later we reached our destination: a beautiful, treeless grassy plateau from which we had a 270 degree view of the south eastern side of Port Dick Arm. We quickly unloaded our packs and set up our 60x spotting scope. We picked an area several miles distant and began our search. We quickly spotted a flock of twenty or so but soon determined that they were nannies and kids- no billies. Over the next hour we viewed another hundred goats but nothing interesting.

We then decided to pack up and head for the small ridge that comprised the remaining 90 degrees that we had no view around. We topped the ridge in an hour and soon discovered that we were in billy country! With the binoculars we could see several fair sized ones. Putting the spotting scope on them, however, revealed none that would meet our specs – 10 inches in length or better. Darkness was fast approaching so we decided to head for camp and return the following day.

The next morning appeared cold, gray and threatening. As we were preparing our meager breakfast it started to rain again- this time in earnest – not a light drizzle but a steady downpour. We had no choice but to head for our tent, dragging behind us what shouldn't get wet. The mountain tent was designed for two men, so the ad said, but the two men that they were referring to must have been Ituri Pygmies. With the added gear we had barely enough room to turn over. Steve and I were good friends who became the best of friends for the downpour lasted for two full days. All I can remember of that trial was that I was into Steve for about 200 bucks playing gin for a buck a hand. He was a much better hunter than he was a card player.

When the storm finally lifted we were stiff and achey but ready climb the ridge again in pursuit of a record book goat. By mid morning the sun broke through the low hanging clouds and soon we were greeted with azure blue skies. The temperature was in the mid 40s, perfect for hunting. We decided to try a new spot several hundred yards south west of where we had spotted the average sized goats. We no sooner settled in when Steve exclaimed in a loud whisper: "Holy cow, come see this one!" The lone billy was only 300 yards away downhill from us and busy grazing. After observing him for several minutes we decided that he was definitely a keeper in the 10 inch range.

Steve suggested that he would guide me to the goat from where he was since there were a series of small ridges between us and the goat which would cause me to lose sight of him periodically. When the billy was obscured from my vision Steve would guide me by a series of hand signals. The eyesight of the mountain goat is second only to the Dall Sheep so utmost caution had to be used in the stalk. Slowly I began my descent being careful to keep whatever little hill or hummock I could find between me and my prey.

Every few yards I looked back for the arm signals: right, left, stop. As I approached a large mound, I looked back and Steve gave me an excited stop signal which meant that my prize was just ahead. I eased my way up the mound as quietly as I could and as I reached the top I slowly peered over the top. There he was- a huge grandpa goat barely 50 yards from me. He was angled away from me which I thought would aid me in not being detected. I slowly raised my 30-06 from my kneeling position and without looking my way the goat bolted! Risking a running shot, I placed the crosshairs just ahead of his left shoulder and squeezed the trigger. He fell just short of his escape route, a perpendicular cliff. He was magnificent: 300 plus pounds of muscle and long white hair somewhat resembling a chest type freezer with legs. Upon closer examination I discovered that my trophy had broken off an inch from his left horn, while the right one was intact and measured exactly 10 inches. It wouldn't make the record book as such but he certainly made my book!

We were greeted by a gorgeous sunset as we finished caping out the goat. It would make a beautiful wall mount, even with a broken horn. We realized after securing the meat to our packs that part of our trek back to camp would be by starlight for we had forgotten our flashlights back at camp. We could barely make out the grassy knoll below us where the camp was but there was a lot of country between.

A light drizzle began as we started our descent and most of the time we were hugging the mountainside for fear of falling forward. We soon realized that somehow in the dark we had strayed off the route we had taken earlier. Inch by inch we sought to find a toehold on the wet rocks. It was getting decidedly colder and our hands were getting numb from feeling the rocks for a handhold. After what seemed like hours, we reached the bottom of the steep mountainside and found our familiar trail back to camp.

Sipping tea early the next misty morning Steve and I both looked back at the mountainside route we had taken the prior night and were amazed that we had made it without incident. Steve, being a devout Christian, was quick to give credit to whom it was due: "Thank God", he said. My unbelieving heart offered no argument.

Chapter Three

My First Moose

It was the winter of 1968 and my first chance at bagging an animal that to me was a trophy animal but to the seasoned Alaskan would be a "staple for the table"- a moose. It was part of the 2nd season, the first being in September/ October. Hunting, with snow on the ground, would be much easier-colder but the visibility would be greater. I was again relying on the relative experience of my partner Ron who by this time had three years of moose hunting under his belt.

We would use his newly acquired Aeronca Chief aircraft as our means of transportation. Its rather mild 65 HP and meager payload of 460 lbs., cruise speed of 105 mph and a range of 200 miles did not place us in the range of super- equipped hunters. However, we were very thankful to have a plane for most other hunters did not have that privilege.

We decided to hunt the area near the confluence of the Yentna and Susitna Rivers some 30 minutes north of Anchorage. Ron had fished the area earlier in the year and had spotted some decent bulls from the air. He was a little skeptical of the choice of my rifle: a 300 Savage with a 180 grain bullet and a peep sight to boot. I assured him that it had killed its share of white tails in Pennsylvania and it could do the job. Ron reminded me that a bull moose would easily outweigh a good white tail by a thousand pounds. Undaunted, I stuck with the Savage.

Dawn greeted us with a temperature of minus 20 and a surreal display of hoar frost, covering the trees with a crystalline sugar coating. When the rays of the rising sun struck the frosty crystals, the resulting awesome display of refracted light seemed to dissipate the sub zero cold. After a routine check for frozen fuel lines and other things unique to the far north, we were on our way down frozen Lake Hood. The skis whistled over the ice and judging the distance we covered for takeoff, the return trip with a load of moose meat would be challenging. A frigid half hour later we reached our hunting area.

The temperature in the plane was nearly that of the outside; we hoped that the later day would bring a more hospitable temperature of zero or better. Ron brought the craft to 500 feet so we could get a closer look at the game. There was a willow covered island at the mouth of the Yentna comprising a hundred acres or so and looked to be "moosey." A single pass revealed a lone bull bedded down in the deep snow.

He seemed to be in the 60 inch class, although antler size was of less importance than how much meat he could offer. I was dropped off 200 yards south of the island in the middle of the frozen Susitna River while Ron buzzed the island hoping to spook the moose into breaking free of the island. A couple of low passes over the moose did the trick; the bull broke from the willow cover and headed for the shore about 200 yards away. He was trotting and covering an amazing amount of ground in a short time. I instinctively knelt, placed the dot in the peep sight just ahead of his front shoulder, and squeezed the trigger. Shocked, I saw him fold immediately and slide nose- first on the river ice.

Now the real work began. This was my first attempt at dressing out a moose, but I assumed that it would be the same as a whitetail, only on a much larger scale. The bull appeared to be a 5 or 6 year old and weighed in at 1000 to 1200 pounds. The antlers measured 58 inches, no trophy by most estimates, but certainly one to me. The job was hampered by the sub zero temperature which caused the blood from the animal to freeze to our hands.

It was messy beyond my expectations but after an hour or so, both of us working together, we had the animal, gutted, skinned and quartered. Now to get the meat back home. As daylight was short at this time of year, we had to move quickly. We decided that Ron would load up as much of the meat into the plane, leave me behind for the second trip, make the 30 minute trip to Lake Hood then return for me and the rest of the meat.

As I watched the plane disappear toward Anchorage I felt alone…very alone. Then the "would ifs" started, and if nurtured might have blazed into panic. I chose another route: to build a fire. I headed to the shore where there would be an abundance of fire wood. Within a few minutes I had a healthy blaze going. My years as a Boy Scout in Pa. were beginning to pay off: I had learned to start a fire almost anywhere. It was first time at being solitary in Alaska. The silence seemed to be deafening- no cars, dogs, kids, or snow blowers-just the occasional squawk of a raven waiting for his share of the kill.

I could hear my heart pounding in my head. As I was drinking in the beauty surrounding me, I heard the faint hum of an aircraft in the distance. As it drew closer, I could see it wasn't Ron; the pilot dipped his wings and seemed to say goodbye. Where could Rod be? He was an hour past schedule. After another half hour of worrying, I heard the familiar drone in the distance and soon Ron was taxiing the Chief near me and our load. Ron informed me that he had run into some ice fog leaving Lake Hood posing some problems for him. Ice fog refers to moisture in the air that, under certain conditions, will freeze and remain airborne for a period of time reducing visibility to nearly zero.

Darkness was rapidly approaching as we hurriedly packed the remaining moose meat into the plane. We knew that we would be exceeding the safe payload limit, but another trip that day was out of the question. We were able to tightly pack everything into the plane except the antlers; they would have to be tied to a wing strut. All was in order for the take off. Ron nosed the overweight craft into the wind and we held our breath. Slowly the Chief slid and bounced down the frozen river's surface until reaching the required airspeed to get us airborne. We were soon flying with the speed of a frozen sea gull but at least we were off the ground.

Ron soon, in his usual calm voice, announced that he was having trouble controlling the craft; it was pitching from side to side erratically. I shouted to Ron: "Do you think it has anything to do with that moose antler tied to the strut?" To which he tersely replied: "Yuh think?" It was apparent that the flight would continue with 3 wings on an aircraft designed to fly with two. I promised to go to church on Sunday.

My pilot did a marvelous job flying the craft for the next half hour. As we came to the mouth of the Susitna River we were shocked to see the Knik Arm between us and Anchorage completely immersed in ice fog! We would try to fly over it. We couldn't see anything through it so the next move would be to fly under the ice fog. We descended through the frozen cotton candy hoping to see the ground before it saw us. We were able to see a rivulet about 300 feet below us and kept that for a reference point.

Ron then began to circle that spot while my job was to try to spot any lights from Anchorage that could guide us home. After about 10 minutes of that maneuver I began to experience vertigo causing me to lose sense of what was up or down- glad I was not the pilot! Ron leveled out for a few seconds, until I could recover then continued to circle. Suddenly, there it was- a faint red light shining through a hole in the fog. I directed Ron to it and immediately we began to fly toward the light.

A short minute later we were flying over the Anchorage Westward Hotel, 14 stories tall with a red light on its roof! There was not enough visibility to attempt to fly

VFR (visual flight rules) directly to Lake Hood so we would have to fly VHR (visual highway rules). Flying at 300 feet we were able to follow the street lights on "C" St. to Northern Lights Blvd. and fly right which would in turn take us to our destination, Lake Hood.

We were greeted by some angry FAA officials asking us what the ---- we thought we were doing flying in ice fog at 300 feet! Neither my pilot nor I were in the mood for any questions so I simply replied that we were late for dinner and our wives were waiting for us. As we loaded everything into the back of our truck I could hear one of the officials exclaim to the others: "Hey guys come here and see what they have tied to the wing strut!" The FAA men gracefully agreed to meet with us a few days later to sort out some possible violations. Later that evening we heard on the local news that the ice fog had claimed 2 aircraft with 4 lives. One flew into Cook Inlet and the other ran out of fuel waiting for the fog to clear.

We all went to church that Sunday.

Chapter Four

My First Caribou

November of 1967 found me on my first big game hunt in Alaska. Fresh up from Pennsylvania, I was more than eager to shoot something of note, which was reason for moving to the Last Frontier. My choice of fare was caribou which is considered by many to be the finest tasting Alaskan game animal excluding, of course, the Dall Sheep. My hunting partners were Ron Sturgeon, mentioned elsewhere in this book, and Fred Abbott, a GI friend enlisted at Ft. Richardson, living off base and a next door neighbor of mine.

Ron had a couple of caribou hunts under his belt having arrived in Alaska in 1963 so he was chosen to be our guide. The hunting area chosen was Lake Louise, located about 180 miles east of Anchorage, 20 miles off the Glen Highway. The Nelchina Caribou Herd, comprised of about 50,000 animals, was indigenous to the area. To the uninformed it sounds like a large herd but it was, in fact, the smallest of the herds in Alaska.

The weather in Anchorage on the day of our departure was clear and in the 30s, perfect for a hunt. My choice of hunting gear was traditional Pa. gear for November: long johns, wool socks, small game leather boots, canvas pants and jacket, a Woolrich shirt, a canvas hat, and wool gloves. My rifle was trusty 300 Savage with a 180 grain bullet with a peep sight to boot. Feeling well equipped as the others did we headed east toward Lake Louise. We made good time in Ron's new Chevy station wagon, despite the icy highway, arriving at the site about 5 hours later along with a few dozen other hunters. Since the sun would set in late afternoon we decided to eat our cold sandwiches and drink whatever was in our Thermoses while it was still light enough.

As the sun was setting we remarked at how cold it had become. A large thermometer in the parking lot revealed that it was now 10 degrees below zero and was sure to drop over night. We unrolled our double GI sleeping bags issued to Ron and I by the Alaska National Guard and Fred unrolled his Army issued single sleeping bag. A few denigrating remarks were made the unpreparedness of the Army and no rebuttal was offered. We crawled into the back of the wagon and were thankful to be out of the weather. Ron and I were soon asleep in our cozy nests but not the case for poor Fred. Waking us up, he informed us that he was freezing as evidenced by his shaking.

We placed Fred between us and hugged him like a Teddy Bear, or Freddy Bear should I say. He soon stopped shaking and we all were soon able to endure the rest of the frigid night in relative comfort. Awaking the next morning the inside of the wagon was frosted over from freezing breath. The temperature had settled in at 30 below. We reluctantly donned our hunting apparel and the hunt was on. The sun rose by mid morning so there would be at least some illusion of warmth.

It only took a short time for me to realize that my clothing was woefully inadequate for the hunt. I had no choice but to keep moving- all day. I hoped someone would bag a caribou quickly so we could abort this overly ambitious folly. Ron and Fred were dressed somewhat better than I so they decided to pick a good spot and wait for the hunters on snow mobiles to drive some animals their way. I heard a few shots crack across the small lake near us and decided to investigate. Covering the several hundred yards warmed me to the point where I could at least stop for a few minutes and assay the situation.

A few minutes later a few more shots were fired within several hundred yards. Soon two snow mobiles appeared dragging caribou behind them. Shucks I thought, they shot theirs and scared the rest away. As I was ready to give up a lone young bull appeared out of nowhere. He was only 50 yards away and had not seen me. I waited until he was looking away then carefully placed a shot where I thought his heart was. He dropped instantly. The Savage had done its job once more.

I didn't think that it was possible to sweat at 20 something below, but after gutting the caribou and dragging him ¾ of a mile I was pretty damp. The first inclination is to remove some clothing but that can be disastrous since the damp clothing can freeze quickly when exposed to the frigid air. It turned out that my caribou was the only one that we bagged that day but it was in true Alaskan style we divided 3 ways. As I was writing this, Ron called me from his new bride's home in Pa. and we had a chance to relive this adventure of 45 years ago. He related to me that he will be living in Pa. for the winters but will spend the summers in Alaska fishing. Well, somebody has to do it! May God bless you Ron.

Chapter Five

The Hurricane Bear

Sadie Cove is a small 4 mile long jewel- like arm of water curling to the south east like an umbilical cord from its mother, Kachemak Bay, home of the picturesque village of Homer on the south end of the fabled Kenai Peninsula. Kachemak, in the Native tongue, means "waters of smoke" derived from the frequent presence of burning coal fires emanating from deep within the strata of the surrounding mountains. Homer was named for an early 1900s pioneer, Homer Pennock, who founded the town as a coal shipping port.

The year 1968 was a banner year for my hunting adventures in Alaska and I had decided to cap off a very successful year with a black bear hunt. In that year I had bagged a Boone and Crockett sheep and a trophy goat. The season for hunting blackies was approaching the end as it was now early October and the bears would soon be hibernating- digging in for the winter. Fortunately for us the bears would hopefully be on their last and biggest feeding binge for the year, fattening up for their winter sleep.

My partner for this hunt was Fred Pahler, a barber from Anchorage and a native of Colorado who had done some hunting in his native state. This had to be a quick hunt for we planned on leaving Anchorage after work on Friday and driving the 250 miles to Homer, spending the night then taking Fred's boat the 6 miles across the bay to Sadie Cove on Saturday, bagging our bears then returning on Sunday; quite an ambitious undertaking for a couple of Cheechakos (greenhorns).

Saturday dawned all too early and after a typical "sourdough" breakfast of sourdough bread, of course, aged bacon and eggs from who knows where, we left the roadhouse and melted into the early morning mist. There was a bone-chilling dampness in the air, typical for the coastal towns on the Kenai, that begged us to retreat back to the warm confines of the roadhouse with its cozy log fireplace. But that was not to be for our adrenaline was already pumping warming us at the thoughts of pursuing the prized black bear!

As soon as daylight permitted we eased the boat trailer into the clear and icy waters of the bay. The water was calm, almost too calm- not unusual, however, for this time of the day. It was normal, later in the day, for the wind to pick up, drafting down the valley from upper Kachemak Bay. As we entered the 16 foot boat it seemed to suddenly shrink in comparison to the 30 and 40 footers anchored near us. The 16 inch or so draft of our vessel seemed rather inadequate too. Oh well, we'll upscale next year! A few yanks on the cord of the aged 25 horse Mercury outboard motor and were off to a pretentious start. Sadie Cove, here we come! After consulting our nautical map we determined that our voyage would take about 45 minutes to an hour barring any unforeseen difficulties.

As we entered the narrow entrance of the bay the early morning fog started to dissipate and we were soon able to start glassing the sides of the mountains for bears. Neither of us had ever been there before; we were speechless at the pristine beauty of the unfolding scene: clear, glassy waters with a slight shade of azure; verdant green mountains capped with sparkling snow rising to several thousand feet from the wet, slippery, rocky beaches. There were no buildings there; no other humans. The cosmopolitan dust was starting to fall off us and we were now exposed and vulnerable to the enchantment of this mystical place. We were soon shaken out of this trance of nature's beauty by the reality of why we were in Sadie Cove: to hunt bears!

We lifted our binoculars and were soon amazed at the numbers of bears that were in our view. They were all above tree line in the verdant grassy meadows, feeding. As we slowly cruised up one shore then the other, covering the length of the Cove, we were able to count 105 black bears and one lonely brown bear. I had never heard of such numbers, before or since that time. It was a harbinger of what was to come. The bears were very busy feeding on what we soon discovered was an unbelievable harvest of mountain blueberries. Bears can be veritable "berry picking machines"; by projecting their lower lip they can literally scoop the berries into their waiting mouth at a prodigious rate.

The mountain berries grow on very short bushes, not more than a foot or so tall, but produce berries in such quantity as to defy belief. During berry time the mountain slopes on the Kenai turn into bluish- purple carpets spread at the feet of the majestic snow crowned peaks. All this grandeur must be stored in the files of my mind's eye, however, for of all things to leave behind- it was our cameras. The files are clear, however, and hopefully will remain that way. We scanned the shoreline looking for a sheltered place to beach our craft, in the event that dangerous unpredictable winds might blow in. It would take some time since the mountains for the most part made a precipitous entry into the waters.

We finally, after about an hour of searching, found a spot at the head of the bay. We secured the boat, taking the rising tide into consideration, donned our backpacks and rifles and headed up the very steep mountain side. We soon found a game trail which normally makes climbing easier, but this trail was covered with a slippery blue slime that turned out to be bear scat. Progress was impossible as we found ourselves slipping and falling into the mess after every few steps.

Killing a bear was not to be that easy even though we were soon to be surrounded by them. Had the bears actually laid an ingenious trap for us? Would we soon be the hunted ones? We soon forfeited the luxury of the " blueberry pie filling" trail and decided to blaze our own trail. Thankfully, the mosquito season was over and all we had to contend with was the profuse growth of "Devil's Club."

Avoiding it as best we could, within an hour we found ourselves above tree line and entering into the first of the feeding meadows. Because of the steepness of the terrain it was difficult to see more than a few hundred feet ahead of us, therefore keeping the scores of bears out of our view! Under those circumstances it would be very difficult to stalk within range given their incredible sense of smell. We would find a spot with the best view possible and wait for them. Since we were sitting in the middle of their 'dining room table" it was only a matter time before they would come our way.

The wind off Kachemak soon started to kick up and despite the chill we hunkered down as best we could and began our wait. Within an hour a feeding bruin appeared straight up the mountain from us about 40 yards away. He had a long shiny prime coat and was in the 250 to 300 lb. class. I chose to let Fred take the first bear for there would, I thought, be more choices later in the day. I coached Him to wait until the bear turned broadside then let him have it in the "boiler house".

Soon there was a loud crack from Fred's 270 and the bear instantly collapsed and started to roll down the steep hillside directly toward us. Not knowing if the bruin was dead yet, I yelled at Fred to get out the way. The rolling bear came to rest a bare 6 feet from us- dead. Fred's shot was accurate and pierced the bear's heart causing a quick expiration. It was a magnificent animal, a male in his prime with a long luxurious coat which would eventually make a beautiful floor rug. As the wind increased and the clouds began to roll in we wasted no time skinning out the creature and removing his back straps for eating.

Since it was late in the afternoon and it was evident that a storm was closing in fast we decided to stake camp later be concerned with dinner. The tent of choice, providentially, was a military   2 man alpine type that theoretically could handle any storm. It would soon be given its ultimate test. No sooner had we finished staking down the tent that we heard a roar from higher in the mountains above us, a roar not unlike that of a jet plane on take -off. It was eerie as well as frightening. We quickly decided to climb into the shelter of the tent. The first gust was probably in the 50mph range and shook the tent considerably. That was nothing compared to what was to follow.

Each succeeding series of gusts increased in power and soon the gusts soon became a steady blow. The tent, despite being solidly staked down, started to lift off the ground as if by some unknown hand. Fortunately, the tent was equipped with sets of canvas loops sewn around the inside perimeter, obviously designed for our purposes. Fred and I assumed spread eagle positions across the tent, grabbed the loops and hung on for dear life. The hurricane force winds continued throughout the sleepless night. Early in the morning the wind subsided and we warily peeked out of the tent.

There was a slight breeze blowing, a pale reminder of the previous night. We were starving since we had no meal the last evening and looked for our cooking gear but, alas, it was nowhere to be found. It no doubt had been carried off by the wind and was probably over the mountain. I hurriedly gathered bits of firewood and soon had a cooking fire going; sufficient to roast the bear back straps, aka "bruin filet mignon." We devoured all the filets and followed that with a dessert of fresh blueberries; who could ask for more? After fleshing out the bear hide and packing what was left of our gear we started the steep descent to the water where we would hopefully find our boat. The descent was more difficult than the ascent since the bluish bear dung that we encountered on the way up was now mixed with the rainwater from the storm and had morphed into an incredibly slimy blue ooze. By the time we reached the beach our "blue jeans" were even bluer and the smell was only tolerable to the local bears. Amazingly, our petite craft was undamaged and only a few feet higher up on the beach than when we left it.

Sadie Cove greeted us with just a slight chop of a foot or two. Not knowing what was ahead we felt a little like Thor Hyerdahl launching the Kon Tiki. We were soon motoring relatively smoothly toward the mouth of the cove. What we saw as we approached Kachemak Bay was enough to scare seaworthy men let alone us "land lubbers." The bay was covered with whitecaps, some in the 5 to 6 foot range, formidable for our 16 foot boat with hardly a 2 foot draft. Nonetheless, we cautiously entered the bay and tried to keep the bow headed into the waves. Soon we were looking up at the waves and feared that we would be swamped.

I yelled at Fred to turn back but he being the captain over ruled and informed me that it would be disastrous to do so. We had no choice but to sail on and hope for the best. It seemed the further we progressed across the bay the more violent the sea became; we were now taking on water, strange bits of flotsam and lots of seaweed. As the water rose in the boat I frantically tried bailing with a small tin can. Suddenly, the motor sputtered to a stop; it was then that, as I had read about, my life passed before me: I saw myself as a young boy, then a man of 28- too young to die. Too young to die; that thought seemed to breathe hope into me and somehow I knew that we were going to make it.

Just then Fred gave the starter cord another yank and the soaked little engine found new life and sputtered into action. After another 2 hours of harrowing navigation we pulled into port in Homer and were immediately met by 2 Coast Guard officials. They alerted us that the port was closed and no one was to leave. We informed them that we were not leaving but were arriving from Sadie Cove. That was impossible they said for our craft was far too small for the venture. After seeing our bear and catching our unfamiliar odor they were convinced and remarked that Someone had been watching out for us. We didn't argue. Neither one of us had much to say on the drive back to Anchorage for we knew that we were 2 very "lucky" hunters. I was thanking Someone who I had not come to know yet, but He was certainly there.

Chapter Six

My Last Hunt in Alaska

It was now the fall of 1977 and life had taken on a new meaning and direction for me. The details of that are explained later on in my testimony. By this time I knew that my time in Alaska was short and I wanted to get one more good hunt in. I was blessed to have two friends who were willing to accompany me: my pastor, Don Smith, of my home church, the Homer Assembly of God Church and elder, Don French. Pastor was a rolley-polley, good-natured fellow who hailed from Idaho and was the veteran of dozens of hunts in his native state.

I had by this time heard countless tales of his deer and elk hunts. His fervor for hunting and fishing was only surpassed by his love for the Lord. Don French had become a close friend and had spent considerable time guiding me through my "spiritual minefield" that is common to many new believers. When I had left the Alaska Pipeline earlier that year Don took me on as an apprentice sheet rocker. Don owned his own sheet rock business and was an amazing craftsman despite his physical handicaps. He was born with a withered left hand and left foot and suffered with a detached retina. In spite of those things he was well known for being the best at that trade in the area. To offset his limitations Don invented many clever tools that later showed up on the market for which he took no credit.

In September we packed all of our hunting and camping gear into Don's 1962 International Harvester 2 1/2 ton box truck and headed north out of Homer to the Denali Highway some 400 miles distant to hunt caribou. My previous Fish and Game experience was paying off for I knew of many prime caribou hunting areas one of them being the Valdez Creek area located about 20 miles to the east of Cantwell on the George Parks Highway.

The trip was rough but the old IH was holding together well, a credit to the many hours of Don's repair work. We reached the creek near evening after a full day of traveling and were ready for a hot meal and a good night's rest. Don was faithful to pack about 5 days of rations for us; I don't remember exactly what we dined on that evening but I do remember a lot of methane engulfing our sleeping quarters that night. No one claimed sole responsibility for the act so true to the hunter's pact we all shared the honors.

The next morning dawned crisp and clear with the temperature in the 30s- perfect for the hunt ahead. After a quick breakfast of Canadian bacon, farm fresh Alaskan eggs and sourdough coffee we embarked up the trail/ road that followed Valdez Creek. The "road" was little more than a tractor trail that served as a haul road for the Valdez Creek Gold Mine operated by the Denali Mining Corporation. The mine had been in operation since 1903 with brief interruptions during WW1 and WW2.

Operations had slowed considerably while we were there and saw no traffic on the road but we did hear activity several hundred yards away. Our progress up the road was slow, having to ford several streams and traverse dozens of mud holes, some of which would have mired the truck had it not been for the 4-wheel drive. After climbing a couple of miles up the mountain we reached a plateau above tree line from which we could glass the mountain for signs of caribou.

The area was prime habitat for the migrating Denali herd; water was abundant as was the caribou's favorite food: reindeer moss, a type of lichen which is native to much of Alaska. It is amazingly rich in nutrients and is able to sustain the animals through the long frigid winters. We parked the truck and turned our attention to the area about midway up the mountain side where there appeared to be some old caribou trails which the caribou will traditionally use year after year.

Within minutes we spotted a small herd of about 25 animals, all bulls of various sizes. Since the rut, or mating season, was approaching it was normal to see males gathered together, probably discussing their courting plans. Our plan was not just to put some meat on the table but to shoot a couple of trophy bulls. To determine if there were any large bulls in the herd would require us to get a lot closer – so our stalk began.

By midmorning the temperature had soared to the low 50s causing us to sweat profusely due to the steep climb. We chose to climb up a semidry creek bed which afforded us some cover from the very sharp eyes of the caribou. When we guessed that we were in the vicinity of the herd we carefully climbed out of the stream bed and warily peered around us while on our bellies. Don and I quickly spotted two large bulls which were sparring, clashing their enormous antlers together. Pastor Don meanwhile decided to take another route in search of some camp meat.

As the two bulls continued sparring we noticed that although both were considered trophies one had a considerably larger rack, perhaps in the record book class. Don asked me which one each of us should shoot and I told him to shoot the one on the right and I would take the one the left (the smaller one), hoping that they would not switch places while we positioned to shoot. We both fired in tandem, my 30-06 and his 308, and both animals crumpled simultaneously. When the whoopees subsided we climbed the 75 yards to where the dead caribou lay and were amazed at their size, each weighing about 300+ pounds. The racks were very impressive; guessing mine to score about 300 Boone and Crockett points and Don's close to 400 points perhaps placing it in the record book.

Pastor heard the shooting came running across the landscape as fast as his short legs could carry him. (I hope you can tell by now that I was very fond of my pastor). After mutually admiring the magnificent beasts the arduous task of skinning and quartering them began. This is where Pastor's years of experience came in handy enabling us to finish the job in about two hours dividing the meat and antlers into six equal piles which meant we would have to make two trips back to the truck. By now we decided that it was time for a brief snack and siesta in the warm 60 degree sunshine.

Reclining on our backpacks we enjoyed the superb view of the upper Susitna River Valley. Our siesta was interrupted by the drone of a small aircraft that seemed to flying in our direction, slowly circling as it proceeded. I commented that the plane looked like a Fish and Game aircraft and they seemed to looking for something. As this was transpiring I noticed that a small cloud had formed over the distant Susitna River, perhaps 2 or 3 miles away, and was slowly but surely moving our way. The Fish and Game patrol plane was steadily circling and moving in our direction apparently not spotting us yet. The cloud seemed to pick up speed and soon rose up the mountain and was strangely stationed directly above us shielding us from the view of the plane. We could hear the drone of the plane a few hundred feet above us but out our sight because of the cloud. Realizing that it was futile to observe us the plane soon left the area leaving us wondering why we were the subject of their scrutiny.

Then came the arduous task of shouldering the backpacks, each weighing about 75 pounds, down the mountain. The trip down was uneventful and even a bit enjoyable just being there in the beautiful environment. After resting a bit we noticed that it was now late afternoon and we would have to hurry in order to get the meat out before nightfall. This was not an area that you would want to be out at night in with a backpack full of bloody meat for this was prime grizzly country! We climbed hard and reached the meat just as the sun was setting.

What a beautiful sight it was watching the sun set over the not-too-distant Susitna River.

We quickly donned our packs and headed down the mountain with the little daylight we had left; it was now September and the days were growing short. I had the heaviest pack and started to drop back from the two packers in front of me.

The light was fading fast and I soon found myself walking down the now- familiar dry streambed. Walking became increasing difficult and soon I was stumbling over the granite boulder in the streambed. I yelled out to the guys to bring me a flashlight but I received no answer, so I cautiously stumbled on, trying to feel my way with a walking stick. Then I heard a rock being turned over 20 yards or so behind me.

It must be the guys I thought! "Is that you Pastor, is that you Don?" I queried. There was no answer. A light wind blew down the creek carrying with it the unmistakable scent of a grizzly! My years as a game warden had exposed me to the various and distinctive smells of the Alaskan animals so this one was not unfamiliar. I froze; my instinct was to drop the pack of meat and run, which would have been the smart thing to do.

God blessed me with above average intelligence but that did not always equate to being smart, i.e. wise, therefore I did not drop the meat and run but rather decided to protect what was rightfully mine, not fully realizing that the 30-06 on my shoulder would be of little value in the dark. With new found courage I yelled at the bear to back off, the caribou was mine! Pastor Don had recently taught me that when overcome with fear or you find yourself in a really tight spot use your "prayer language". So there I went down the stream speaking and praying in "unknown tongues" with all my might. It was probably an unknown language to another human but perhaps not to that grizzly for soon after I started praying I heard not another sound from him and the BO (bear odor) dissipated. I soon rejoined my companions and they related that they were praying for me and I replied, "me too!" There was cause for much rejoicing around the campfire that night.

The next morning, after a hearty breakfast highlighted by caribou steaks, we aimed the truck toward the Denali Highway. After fording a couple of streams we noticed an old cabin along the trail with some smoke coming from the chimney that seemed to say "welcome." A knock on the old planked door was followed by a "come on in." Seated across the one room cabin was a wizened old man sipping a cup of miner's coffee, fit only for the most hardened of coffee drinkers.

He offered us a seat on a couple of rough sawn wooden benches and a cup of his brew which we gladly accepted. A little wary of these "drop- in – visitors" at first, he quickly lightened up when he realized that we were church folk. Our conversation eventually turned to him and what he was doing alone in such a remote area. He eagerly explained that he had been in that area for several years and was a gold panner who had an agreement with the mining company to "clean up after them.";" which meant that after they were finished sluicing an area of the stream he would come in after them and pan for the gold that they hopefully left behind.

We asked him if it was a lucrative venture for him and he replied that it was "ok." He then asked if we would like to see some of his "flour gold" which is finest grade of gold that one can pan and looks like golden flour. He reached under his bed and produced a quart jar of the precious mineral. I estimated the jar to weigh about 50 pounds which by today's standards would be worth about 960,000 dollars! He then produced a quart of "wheat gold" (small gold particles resembling grains of wheat). Then finally he produced a quart of small nuggets which he sold as jeweler's gold, the most valuable. I'm sure he had more stashed away but that was enough to satisfy our covetous eyes for that day!

He then asked us what brought us to the area and we replied that we came to hunt caribou and had found some success. He asked to see the animals and we readily acquiesced. After admiring the animals we offered him a few steaks and he was pleased to accept them saying that it had been a while since he had fresh meat. He then informed us that it was illegal to use vehicles to hunt in the area. We checked the game regulation book and found him to be correct. Embarrassed, we apologized, offered him more meat and headed for the highway before Fish and Game returned. That explained why the plane was circling us but we still have no explanation for the cloud that mysteriously appeared and hid us.

My Testimony

I was raised as a good Catholic boy in the steel town of Lyndora, Pennsylvania nestled in the foothills of Western Pennsylvania. I went to church faithfully each Sunday and religiously partook of the sacraments. I felt an authentic connection with God and at times forsook the things of this world just to spend time with Him. Sadly, that relationship faded as I entered my teen years. There were too many allurements to pass up: girls, cars, Carlings Black Label, and girls; no weed though; those were the BP days- Before Pot.

By the time I was 18 the Lord was just a fond memory- but He had me on His mind. I could have gotten into a lot of trouble during those days. Some of my friends did hard time at Rockview State Penitentiary but I just happened to not be with them when they did the bad stuff. What really saved me (besides praying grandmothers) was my love for the outdoors. Hunting and fishing was in my DNA; thanks to Dad.

After 3 years at Penn State enrolled in a myriad of mundane courses I was bored beyond endurance. Early one morning as I was getting ready for classes I heard a familiar sound outdoors. Drawn by some unseen force I ran out of the dorm and there to my extreme delight was a flock of Canadian Geese, flying in formation heading north. Something inside summoned me to head north as the geese. I must go to Alaska- I had delayed long enough. I withdrew from college much to the disappointment of my Dad, but he was soon pacified by the fact that I would be headed to his secret love denied- Alaska.

In retrospect, I could see God orchestrating my plans but I didn't recognize it at the time. I was being blessed by Him but gave the credit to myself for being a "go getter." My spiritual life was in "limbo", or so I thought, until I had an epiphany on Easter in perhaps 1967. Being a Catholic and feeling guilty for not going to church for a year I chose to make up for it by fulfilling my Easter Duty which was to go to confession then receive Holy Communion on Easter Sunday. Then, in my eyes, I was good for another year!

The man hearing my confession was certainly an unusual looking priest. He didn't have the black garb with the white collar but was dressed in a brown robe and was really young. The background music was kind of cool: a religious cross between Simon and Garfunkel and Bob Dylan. I liked this guy; his tone and demeanor were really laid back. Was he a hippie priest by chance? I wanted to give him the peace sign but he might not see it in the dark confessional.

Why are confessionals always so dark I thought; maybe to hide the really bad sinners like myself. After confessing my sins, which was akin to reading a yearly grocery list, the young priest asked why I was doing that and I replied that I wanted God to know that I had sinned. He said that God already knew that. I then asked what should I then do and he said to repent of my sins. Repent? What does that mean? He did his best to explain it to me but I wasn't ready to make that drastic change of quitting sinning. I was having far too much fun, or so I thought. As I was leaving the confessional I asked him what my penance was and he almost casually said that Jesus did my penance on the cross for me; I just needed to walk in forgiveness. In 10 minutes this Franciscan Monk had severely damaged 25 years of my pseudo- theology! His short but profound doctrinal truths would dwell in the recesses of my mind for the next ten years.

In 1972 after leaving the ADF&G I decided to take a hiatus from The Last Frontier. The disappointment of discovering corruption in the Department which led to my eventual departure left a hole in my heart. My dreams were dashed. My healing, I believed, would come from a change of scenery. Colorado seemed to be the antidote. Hunting and fishing in a different venue had to be the cure. My former employer, Honeywell, Inc., welcomed me back and arranged for a transfer to Denver.

I soon found myself once again immersed in a paradise of hunting and fishing adding Wyoming to my playground. After a little more than a year later I found myself yearning strangely for the Land. One Sunday morning while reading the newspaper I chanced on an article reporting that the building of the Alaska Oil Pipeline was commencing. My healed heart was again being drawn northward. Unknown to me the Creator was sending me back to my home in Alaska.

After spending two years on the Alaska Pipeline stationed at Prudhoe Bay and suffering some bitter disappointments, feeling that my life was going nowhere but down, I had my second epiphany. My best friend, Steve Vir-Gin, invited me aside one evening after dinner at Base Operations Camp and said that he had something to share with me. There was a refreshing excitement in Steve, something that I hadn't seen before. He took out a small Bible and asked if I minded if he read something to me. I rudely asked him if he was a "Jesus Freak" and he promptly answered that he was.

He began to read from the Gospel of John and quite unlike me I was speechless- I literally had nothing to say except "thank you" when he finished. Something deep inside was stirring; it wasn't frightening, in fact, it was comforting. We met for a few days together until it came time for us to depart for home for our alternating week off. After the last day that Steve shared I distinctly heard that inaudible voice of the Spirit beckon me: "Time to come home, son." The prodigal was beckoned home! The Father was readying the banquet and was going to throw a party for his once lost son who was now found. I formalized my commitment to My Heavenly Father through His Son, Jesus Christ, on Jan.13th 1977 at 9:30 PM in the Homer Assembly of God church in Homer, Alaska. I thank the dedicated Pastor there at the time, Pastor Don Smith and his wife, Austa who graciously accepted me into their church home when I had none. I thank the saints there also for their love, acceptance, and forgiveness without which I would not have survived.

Each time that I review this book I am reminded of how faithful God was in the many times that I could have perished. He was there all the time....waiting for me: A King waiting for his subject. Only our King Jesus would do that.

I am currently Pastoral Care Director for New Beginnings Ministry in Clermont, Florida where we provide food, clothing and shelter, as well as job training and Christian Discipleship for homeless men and women. There isn't a day that goes by that the residents don't hear about my adventures in Alaska. In my "spare time" I lead a Messianic Fellowship on the Sabbath. I hope that you will agree with me that God is good and faithful. Throughout all the years in The Last Frontier God was always there for me, and He is there for you too, my friend.

Is 41:10   Fear not, **for I am with you**; be not dismayed, for I am your God; I will strengthen you, I will help you, I will uphold you with my righteous right hand.

He is there even when we're not, for He is faithful.

He is there when we can't feel Him, for He is spirit.

He is there when we sleep, because He never does.

He is there when we reject Him, even though it hurts Him.

He is there when we need Him, even when we say we don't.

He is there when someone breaks our heart, for His was broken too.

He was there when we were born for He is the Alpha, the Beginning, He will be there when we die for He is the Omega, **THE END.**

Epilogue to
Adventures of an Alaskan Game Warden

God continues to be there for me .On the morning of Thursday February 5, 2015 I suffered a cardiac arrest. It came to me as a complete surprise since I work out daily and adhere to a good diet (or so I thought). The cardiac surgeons were able to resuscitate me and install a stent in my Left Descending Aorta (aka the widow maker). Thanks to my Creator, I am recovering well and am impressed to continue and refine my ministry unto Him for as many years as He has planned for me.

The event has been life-changing for me: I have gained a "true perspective" on my life. If I had been taken home in February, I would have been in the presence of the Lord, but He has other plans that I know not of. However, there is one thing that I do know and that is God has a reason for this affliction- for me to be drawn closer to Him and to be fashioned into a holier and more complete child of His. "We shall know Him when we see Him, for we shall be like Him."

My perspective has changed:

I can no longer put off what God has impressed
me to do. No procrastinating!

I must be diligent in every area of my life; this day
may be my last. May I live it to the fullest in accordance
with the Father's will. Therefore, I have committed
myself to love more, laugh more often and live well.

AWH
Minneola, Florida

2/16/2015

MEMORANDUM   State of Alaska

TO: ☐ Alvin W. Huba
Protection Assistant
Anchorage

DATE : December 8, 1970

FROM: Wallace H. Noerenberg
Commissioner
Department of Fish and Game

SUBJECT: Public Safety Training
Academy Course - Sitka

I wish to extend my personal congratulations for your successful completion of the course of study at the Public Safety Training Academy at Sitka this past month.

Due to the press of business following my extensive meetings in Tokyo and California, I was unable to attend the graduation ceremonies. Therefore, I take this opportunity to express my appreciation and thank you for a job well done.

STATE OF ALASKA

KEITH H. MILLER, GOVERNOR

DEPARTMENT OF ADMINISTRATION

DIVISION OF PERSONNEL   POUCH C — JUNEAU 99801

February 19, 1970

Mr. Alvin W. Huba
% Department of Fish & Game
1018 International Airport Rd.
Anchorage, Alaska 99502

Dear Mr. Huba:

Thank you for your assistance in validating the new State Trooper and Protection Assistant II test. The hundreds of hours donated by the test subjects has resulted in what we think is a sound, fair and accurate test. We could not have done it without your help.

We are sending a copy of this letter to the Personnel Officer of your Department to place in your file. In addition, we are placing a copy in your State employee file in our office.

As you know, no comparison is being made of your performance on the job. You may, however, be interested in how you did. Mr. Neil Koeniger in the Anchorage Field Office of the Personnel Division has a list of scores of those who used identification numbers on their answer sheets. You may contact him with your identification number to find out your score.

Very truly yours,

Michael P. McMullen
Personnel Analyst

ANCHORAGE BOROUGH

SCHOOL DISTRICT

OFFICE OF THE SUPERINTENDENT

670 FIREWEED LANE
ANCHORAGE, ALASKA 99503
AREA CODE 907 277-8652

July 24, 1970

Mr. Al Huba
Alaska Department of Fish and Game
Protection Division
212 East International Airport Road
Anchorage, Alaska 99502

Dear Mr. Huba:

On behalf of all those involved in the Outdoor Education
Program, I would like to thank you for your outstanding assistance. This project provided an educational experience to
children who otherwise would not have received this advantage.

Your cooperation and assistance further demonstrates the
great potential that exists through the sharing of talented
people from our professional community.

Again, our sincerest thanks for all the time and effort
you gave to this program.

Sincerely yours,

Joe D. Montgomery
Acting Superintendent

JDM:lp

ARMED SERVICES BRANCH

Young Men's Christian Association

ANCHORAGE, ALASKA 99501

6th and F Street
P.O. BOX 559
Tel. 277-8522

April 6, 1970

Mr. Al Huba
Alaska Dept. of Fish & Game
212 East International Airport Road
Anchorage, Alaska   99502

Dear Mr. Huba:

I would like to personally thank you for all your time and
efforts in assisting the Anchorage Armed Services YMCA with
the Annual Hunting Course for 1970.

Through your efforts and members of your staff some 313 people
were given an opportunity to become more familiar with the
various aspects of Hunting in Alaska.

We sincerely appreciate your time and interest in this program.

Sincerely,

Hal Durham
Executive Director

HD:rfc

SERVING THE ARMED F

The YMCA is a [...]

DEPARTMENT OF THE ARMY
HEADQUARTERS US ARMY, ALASKA SUPPLY CONTROL CENTER (PROVISIONAL)
APO SEATTLE 98749

10 JUN 1970

ARCO

SUBJECT: Letter of Appreciation

Mr. A. W. Huba
Protection Officer
Department of Fish and Game
212 E. International Airport Road
Anchorage, Alaska 99502

1. Please accept my sincere gratitude and appreciation for your courtesy
in supporting the United States Army, Alaska, Summer Safety Campaign for
1970, at Fort Richardson. The presentations you gave to the USARAL Supply
Control Center military and civilian personnel, Wednesday and Thursday, 27
and 28 May 1970, were not only of interest because of their timely nature,
but enjoyable in the method with which they were proffered.

2. It is apparent, from the generous contribution of your time, that you
share a mutual concern with us for the welfare and safety of others. This
was notable in the obvious preparation you made in assembling the information set forth to the members of our organization. You have contributed
markedly toward the success of our seasonal safety program.

3. It was a pleasure to have had the opportunity to meet you. Thank you
again for your consideration and community mindedness expressed on our
behalf.

CHARLES W. McQUEARY
Colonel, TC
Chief, USARAL Supply Control Center

CF: Mr. Wm. R. Martin
    Senior Protection Officer
    Dept of Fish & Game

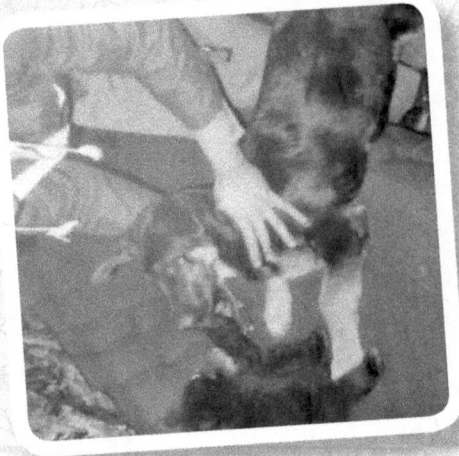

My dog "Deshka" playing with a black bear cub.
1970

Ron & I packing in for sheep.
1968

Al with Boone & Crockett sheep.
1968

1970 graduating class (Al 2nd from left).

Al with morning catch of sockeyes.
1968

Al with meduim sized King Salmon.
1977

Al with trophy mountain goat.
1968

Al & Tim with rams.
1968

Al & "Ol" Pete panning for gold.
1972

Warden Al on TV Show.
1970

A Little Moose Goes Home

MINI-MOOSE MOVED TO MAMA

Al Huba, a protection officer with the Alaska Department of Fish and Game, helps a three-week old moose calf into the back of a station wagon after it was found roaming in Mountain View in the area of Second Avenue and Klevin Street. The calf was in good condition and was released a few miles beyond Ft. Richardson, where its mother had been seen. The Department of Fish and Game has stressed the importance of leaving any stray animals alone and calling the department if a young animal appears to be injured or abandoned.

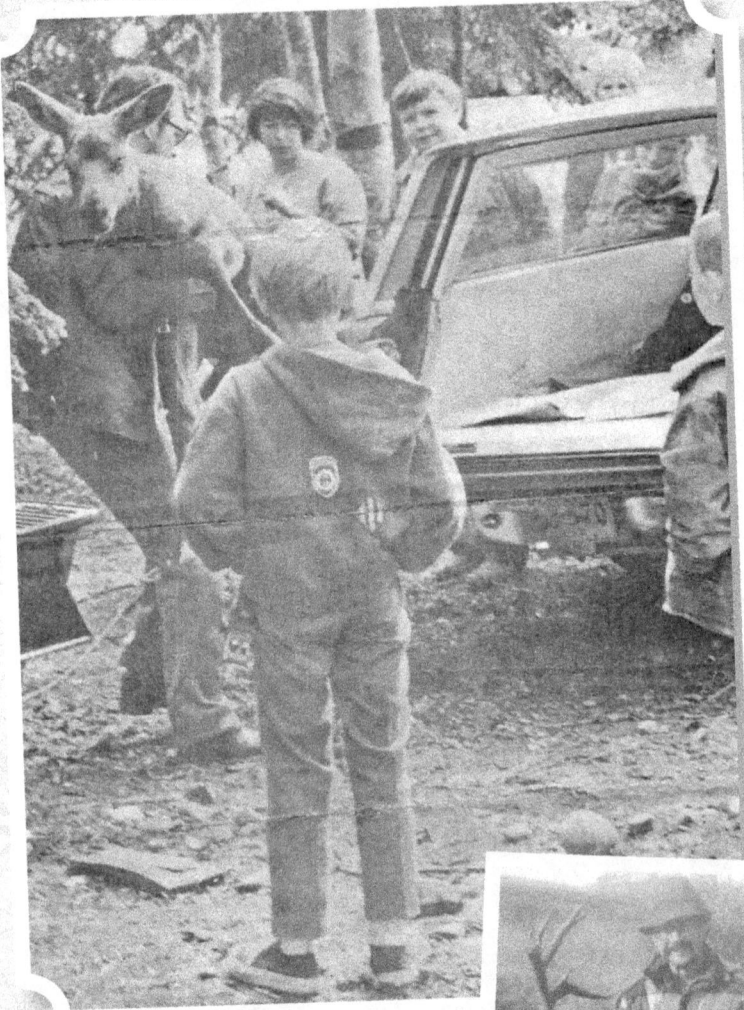

Al's "last hunt caribou".
1977

Al's & son Aaron's 1st King Salmon. 1992

Al on mountain goat hunt. 1968